In Praise of
Goldens

With stories from James Herriot, Dean Koontz, Ted Kerasote,
Roger Welsch, Kenny Salwey, and more

Photographs by Lynn M. Stone

Voyageur Press

First published in 2008 by MBI Publishing Company and Voyageur Press, an imprint of MBI Publishing Company, 400 First Avenue North, Suite 300, Minneapolis, MN 55401 USA

Text copyright © 2008 by Voyageur Press

Photography copyright © Lynn M. Stone, except where noted.

The information in this book is true and complete to the best of our knowledge. All recommendations are made without any guarantee on the part of the author or Publisher, who also disclaim any liability incurred in connection with the use of this data or specific details.

Voyageur Press titles are also available at discounts in bulk quantity for industrial or sales-promotional use. For details write to Special Sales Manager at MBI Publishing Company, 400 First Avenue North, Suite 300, Minneapolis, MN 55401 USA.

To find out more about our books, join us online at www.voyageurpress.com.

Library of Congress Cataloging-in-Publication Data

In Praise of Goldens/ Voyageur Press.
  p. cm.
  ISBN 978-0-7603-3471-3 (hb w/ jkt)
  1. Golden retriever--Anecdotes. I. Voyageur Press.
SF429.G63I67 2008
636.752'7--dc22
                                    2008014425

Editor: Leah Noel
Designer: Chris Fayers

Printed in China

Permissions

We have made every effort to determine original sources and locate copyright holders of the excerpts in this book. Grateful acknowledgment is made to the writers, publishers, and agencies listed below for permission to reprint material copyrighted or controlled by them. Please bring to our attention any errors of fact, omission, or copyright.

"Mrs. Donovan" from *James Herriot's Dog Stories* by James Herriot. Copyright © 1986 by the author and reprinted by permission of St. Martin's Press, LLC. Reprinted in the United Kingdom and Commonwealth by permission of David Higham Associates for Michael Joseph Limited.

"From the Wild" from *Merle's Door: Lessons from a Freethinking Dog* by Ted Kerasote. Copyright © 2007 by Ted Kerasote. Reprinted by permission of Houghton Mifflin Harcourt Publishing Company. Reprinted in the United Kingdom and Commonwealth by permission of the author and the author's agents, Scovil Chichak Galen Literary Agency, Inc.

"Just Like Me" from *The Angel by My Side* by Michael Lingenfelter and David Frei. © 2002 by Michael Lingenfelter and David Frei. Reprinted with permission from Hay House, Inc., Carlsbad, California.

Chapter 13 from *The Darkest Evening of the Year* by Dean Koontz. Copyright © 2007 by Dean Koontz. Used by permission of Bantam Books, a division of Random House, Inc.

"Lady of the House" by Roger Welsch. Copyright © 2008 by Roger Welsch. Reprinted with permission of the author.

"Pack Maneuvers" from *Golden Days: Memories of a Golden Retriever* by Arthur Vanderbilt. Copyright © 1998 by Arthur Vanderbilt. Used by permission of Willow Creek Press.

"Traveling Travis McTavish" by Kenny Salwey. Copyright © 2008 by Kenny Salwey. Reprinted with permission of the author.

"Now Wait a Minute, Chester" by Eric Saperston. Copyright © 2008 by Eric Saperston. Reprinted with permission of the author.

Pages 74–81 from Chapter 6 of *Dog Years* by Mark Doty. Copyright © 2007 by Mark Doty. Reprinted by permission of HarperCollins Publishers.

Additional photo credits

Pages 23, 33, 35: Shutterstock/Joy Brown. Page 144: Shutterstock/Temelko Temelkov. Page 146: Shutterstock/Lisa A. Svara. Page 149: Shutterstock/Sonya Etchison. Backgrounds: Shutterstock/Jeffrey Schmieg

Contents

Introduction

For those who own a golden retriever, it's no secret that this lovable, playful, tail-wagging dog quickly finds a place in your heart. How could anyone not adore such a friendly, gentle creature? Yes, they may not be the world's best guard dog, and their big bushy tail may knock over and break some cherished items in your home, but their charms are overwhelming.

Whether it's snuggling up close on dark, cold nights or joyfully playing catch with a Frisbee in the afternoon sun, a golden always becomes an integral part of the family. No wonder goldens are among the world's foremost pets and consistently rank in the top five of most popular American Kennel Club (AKC) breeds. Some 60,000 golden retrievers are registered with the AKC, with 5,600 more in Canada and 9,400 in the United Kingdom.

With their easygoing and trusting demeanor, golden retrievers are great with kids, always ready to receive love and affection. In fact, anyone who spends the time to establish a positive rapport with a golden will have a friend for life. With their natural intelligence and ability to be easily trained, golden retrievers also make great hunting dogs (a task for which they were originally bred), drug-sniffing dogs, rescue dogs, and therapy dogs. They can learn as many as 240 commands, words, and phrases. They truly are one of mankind's best companions. The breed's description by the AKC as "a symmetrical, powerful, active dog, sound and well put together, not clumsy nor long in the leg, displaying a kindly expression and possessing a personality that is eager, alert, and self-confident" doesn't do it justice.

Goldens have made their homes in the White House (former President Gerald Ford owned a golden named Liberty), the Maharajah of Junagadh, India's palace, and more. Nine Inch Nails frontman Trent Reznor has owned one, so has suspense writer Dean Koontz (whose story about a golden is featured in this book). Goldens also have been faithful friends in many

movies and television shows, including *Air Bud* (the story of a basketball-playing golden retriever), *Homeward Bound*, *Full House, Punky Brewster, The Drew Carey Show*, and *Pushing Daisies*.

No, golden retrievers aren't the perfect dog, but they come close. That's why it's surprising that they have a shorter history with humans than most popular breeds, a history that was a colorful mystery until the 1950s.

A Brief History of the Golden

For many years, golden retrievers were thought to be descendants of a group of Russian circus dogs that Sir Dudley Marjoribanks (also known as the first Lord Tweedmouth) of Guisachan, Scotland, purchased and bred in the mid-1800s. That whimsical tale was debunked, though, in 1952 when the sixth Earl of Ilchester, the great-nephew of Lord Tweedmouth, published his research of his great-uncle's stud book. Nowhere in the meticulous records from 1835 to 1890 was a mention of any Russian dogs.

Instead, the records showed golden retrievers came from mixing a yellow retriever named Nous with a Tweed water spaniel named Belle in 1868. (The Tweed water spaniel is now extinct but is believed to be a strain of the Irish water spaniel with a light, liver-colored coat and close curls.) The goal of the breeding was to produce the ultimate hunting dog—a vigorous, powerful retriever that could travel great distances, sometimes over difficult terrain, to fetch fowl but would also be gentle and easily trainable. The first litter of four pups became the basis of a breeding program that not only included the golden retriever, but eventually the Irish setter, the sand-colored bloodhound, the St. John's water dog of Newfoundland, and two wavy-coated black retrievers.

The British Kennel Club first recognized golden retrievers as a distinct breed, known as "retriever (golden and yellow)," in 1911. Two years later, the Golden Retriever Club of England was formed. The breed's name was officially changed to golden retriever in 1920.

The first golden retrievers imported into North America probably arrived in 1881. The Honorable Archie Marjoribanks, son of Lord Tweedmouth, brought two goldens with him to his ranch in Texas. Meanwhile, his sister, Ishbel Marjoribanks, who was also the wife of the governor general of Canada, was photographed with a golden retriever in Ottawa in 1894. Yet it wasn't until 1927 that a golden was first registered in Canada; the AKC received its first golden retriever registration just two years earlier in 1925. The breed received widespread attention in 1933, when Speedwell Pluto, an imported golden who was described by breeder Ralph Boalt of Winona, Minnesota, as "big, powerful, and courageous," won an American bench championship. The first National Retriever Field Trial champion, a golden called King Midas of Woodend, further solidified the breed's reputation by winning his title in 1941. Since then, golden retrievers have won many show titles and increased greatly in popularity.

In 1932, only twenty golden retrievers were registered with the AKC. By 1964, that number had risen to nearly 4,000. It peaked in the late 1990s with about 70,000 registered golden retrievers in the United States. While that number has dipped by about 10,000 today, the golden retriever is still regarded by many as the world's greatest dog.

About **In Praise of Goldens**

In Praise of Goldens celebrates all that is great about owning a golden, from taking it on meandering scenic walks (as described in Arthur Vanderbilt's excerpt from *Golden Days*) to discovering its true emotional intelligence (highlighted by both Dean Koontz in his piece from *The Darkest Evening of the Year* and Roger Welsch in his essay *Lady of the House*). In the selection from *The Angel by My Side*, Mike Lingenfelter and David Frei tell the story of a rescue dog named Dakota, who provides comfort and lifesaving help in the toughest of times, while author and poet Mark Doty reflects on bringing a golden home to share the last days of his dying partner. Bestselling outdoors writer and author Ted Kerasote relates a tale of a golden mix found living in the wild with a spirit that could not be contained in the human world while Yorkshire veterinarian James Herriot profiles a golden retriever who never loses his faith in humankind despite unimaginable cruelty. Filmmaker Eric Saperston shares his story about taking his golden on a four-year cross-country road trip, and "The Last River Rat" Kenny Salwey's bittersweet essay reflects on the last days of one of his wife's dogs, bringing a tear to the eye of any true golden lover.

All in all, these stories, along with stunning photography from golden owner Lynn M. Stone, give praise where it is due—to the beloved golden retriever, best friend to all.

Chapter 1

An Unbreakable Golden Spirit

Mrs. Donovan

by

James Herriot

The late James Herriot was well into his fifties when he wrote his first memoir of his Yorkshire veterinarian practice. Since the publication of *All Creatures Great and Small* in the 1970s, his wonderful essays and his stories for children have made him one of the most cherished writers of the twentieth century.

Scottish by birth, Herriot practiced veterinary medicine in Yorkshire, where he also wrote most of his books, including *All Things Bright and Beautiful, All Things Wise and Wonderful, The Lord God Made Them All, Every Living Thing*, and *James Herriot's Yorkshire*. His children's books include *Moses the Kitten, Only One Woof*, and *The Market Square Dog*. Herriot always portrayed the animals he wrote about in a humane and loving voice.

This selection originally appeared in *All Things Bright and Beautiful* and was later published in *James Herriot's Dog Stories*. The story features Mrs. Donovan, a dog lover with a kind heart, and the story of Roy—a classic golden who, despite spending his early life in complete neglect, has an unbreakable spirit and is willing to trust a new owner to give him a better life.

*T*he silvery-haired old gentleman with the pleasant face didn't look the type to be easily upset, but his eyes glared at me angrily and his lips quivered with indignation.

"Mr. Herriot," he said, "I have come to make a complaint. I strongly object to your callousness in subjecting my dog to unnecessary suffering."

"Suffering? What suffering?" I was mystified.

"I think you know, Mr. Herriot. I brought my dog in a few days ago. He was very lame, and I am referring to your treatment on that occasion."

I nodded. "Yes, I remember it well . . . but where does the suffering come in?"

"Well, the poor animal is going around with his leg dangling, and I have it on good authority that the bone is fractured and should have been put in plaster immediately." The old gentleman stuck his chin out fiercely.

"All right, you can stop worrying," I said. "Your dog has a radial paralysis caused by a blow on the ribs, and if you are patient and follow my treatment, he'll gradually improve. In fact, I think he'll recover completely."

"But he trails his leg when he walks."

"I know—that's typical, and to the layman it does give the appearance of a broken leg. But he shows no sign of pain, does he?"

"No, he seems quite happy, but this lady seemed to be absolutely sure of her facts. She was adamant."

"Lady?"

"Yes," said the old gentleman. "She is clever with animals, and she came round to see if she could help in my dog's convalescence. She brought some excellent condition powders with her."

"Ah!" A blinding shaft pierced the fog in my mind. All was suddenly clear. "It was Mrs. Donovan, wasn't it?"

"Well . . . er, yes. That was her name."

Old Mrs. Donovan was a woman who really got around. No matter what was going on in Darrowby—weddings, funerals, house-sales—you'd find the dumpy little figure and walnut face among the spectators, the darting, black-button eyes taking everything in. And always, on the end of its lead, her terrier dog.

When I say "old," I'm only guessing because she appeared ageless; she seemed to have been around a long time, but she could have been anything between fifty-five and seventy-five. She certainly had the vitality of a young woman because she must have walked vast distances in her dedicated quest

to keep abreast of events. Many people took an uncharitable view of her acute curiosity, but whatever the motivation, her activities took her into almost every channel of life in the town. One of these channels was our veterinary practice.

Because Mrs. Donovan, among her other widely ranging interests, was an animal doctor. In fact, I think it would be safe to say that this facet of her life transcended all the others.

She could talk at length on the ailments of small animals, and she had a whole armory of medicines and remedies at her command, her two specialties being her miracle-working condition powders and a dog shampoo of unprecedented value for improving the coat. She had an uncanny ability to sniff out a sick animal, and it was not uncommon when I was on my rounds to find Mrs. Donovan's dark gypsy face poised intently over what I

had thought was my patient while she administered calf's foot jelly or one of her own patent nostrums.

I suffered more than Siegfried because I took a more active part in the small animal side of our practice. I was anxious to develop this aspect and to improve my image in this field, and Mrs. Donovan didn't help at all. "Young Mr. Herriot," she would confide to my clients, "is all right with cattle and such like, but he don't know nothing about dogs and cats."

And of course they believed her and had implicit faith in her. She had the irresistible mystic appeal of the amateur, and on top of that, there was her habit, particularly endearing in Darrowby, of never charging for her advice, her medicines, her long periods of diligent nursing.

Older folk in the town told how her husband, an Irish farm worker, had died many years ago and how he must have had "a bit put away" because Mrs. Donovan had apparently been able to indulge all her interests over the years without financial strain. Since she inhabited the streets of Darrowby all day and every day, I often encountered her, and she always smiled up at me sweetly and told me how she had been sitting up all night with Mrs. So-and-so's dog that I'd been treating. She felt she'd be able to pull it through.

There was no smile on her face, however, on the day when she rushed into the surgery while Siegfried and I were having tea.

"Mr. Herriot!" she gasped. "Can you come? My little dog's been run over!"

I jumped up and ran out to the car with her. She sat in the passenger seat with her head bowed, her hands clasped tightly on her knees.

"He slipped his collar and ran in front of a car," she murmured. "He's lying in front of the school halfway up Cliffend Road. Please hurry."

I was there within three minutes, but as I bent over the dusty little body stretched on the pavement I knew there was nothing I could do. The fast-glazing eyes, the faint, gasping respirations, the ghastly pallor of the mucus membranes all told the same story.

"I'll take him back to the surgery and get some saline into him, Mrs. Donovan," I said. "But I'm afraid he's had a massive internal hemorrhage. Did you see what happened exactly?"

She gulped. "Yes, the wheel went right over him."

Ruptured liver, for sure. I passed my hands under the little animal and began to lift him gently, but as I did so the breathing stopped and the eyes stared fixedly ahead.

Mrs. Donovan sank to her knees, and for a few moments she gently stroked the rough hair of the head and chest. "He's dead, isn't he?" she whispered at last.

"I'm afraid he is," I said.

She got slowly to her feet and stood bewilderedly among the little group of bystanders on the pavement. Her lips moved, but she seemed unable to say any more.

I took her arm, led her over to the car, and opened the door. "Get in and sit down," I said. "I'll run you home. Leave everything to me."

I wrapped the dog in my calving overall and laid him in the boot before driving away. It wasn't until we drew up outside Mrs. Donovan's house that she began to weep silently. I sat there without speaking till she had finished. Then she wiped her eyes and turned to me.

"Do you think he suffered at all?"

"I'm certain he didn't. It was all so quick—he wouldn't know a thing about it."

She tried to smile. "Poor little Rex, I don't know what I'm going to do without him. We've travelled a few miles together, you know."

"Yes, you have. He had a wonderful life, Mrs. Donovan. And let me give you a bit of advice—you must get another dog. You'd be lost without one."

She shook her head. "No, I couldn't. That little dog meant too much to me. I couldn't let another take his place."

"Well I know that's how you feel just now, but I wish you'd think about it. I don't want to seem callous—I tell everybody this when they lose an animal, and I know it's good advice."

"Mr. Herriot, I'll never have another one." She shook her head again, very decisively. "Rex was my faithful friend for many years, and I just want to remember him. He's the last dog I'll ever have."

∾

I often saw Mrs. Donovan around the town after this, and I was glad to see she was still active as ever, though she looked strangely incomplete without the little dog on its lead. But it must have been over a month before I had the chance to speak to her.

It was on the afternoon that Inspector Halliday of the RSPCA rang me.

"Mr. Herriot," he said, "I'd like you to come and see an animal with me. A cruelty case."

"Right, what is it?"

"A dog, and it's pretty grim. A dreadful case of neglect." He gave me the name of a row of old brick cottages down by the river and said he'd meet me there.

Halliday was waiting for me, smart and business-like in his dark uniform, as I pulled up in the back lane behind the houses. He was a big, blond man with cheerful blue eyes, but he didn't smile as he came over to the car.

"He's in here," he said, and led the way toward one of the doors in the long, crumbling wall. A few curious people were hanging around, and with a feeling of inevitability I recognized a gnome-like brown face. Trust Mrs. Donovan, I thought, to be among those present at a time like this.

We went through the door into the long garden. I had found that even the lowliest dwellings in Darrowby had long strips of land at the back, as though the builders had taken it for granted that the country people who were going to live in them would want to occupy themselves with the pursuits of the soil—with vegetable and fruit growing, even stock keeping in a small way. You usually found a pig there, a few hens, often pretty beds of flowers.

But this garden was a wilderness. A chilling air of desolation hung over the few gnarled apple and plum trees standing among a tangle of rank grass as though the place had been forsaken by all living creatures.

Halliday went over to a ramshackle wooden shed with peeling paint and a rusted corrugated-iron roof. He produced a key, unlocked the padlock, and dragged the door partly open. There was no window, and it wasn't easy to identify the jumble inside: broken gardening tools, an ancient mangle, rows of flower pots, and partly used paint tins. And right at the back, a dog sitting quietly.

I didn't notice him immediately because of the gloom and because the smell in the shed started me coughing, but as I drew closer I saw that he was a big animal, sitting very upright, his collar secured by a chain to a ring in the wall. I had seen some thin dogs, but this advanced emaciation reminded me of my textbooks on anatomy; nowhere else did the bones of pelvis, face, and rib cage stand out with such horrifying clarity. A deep, smoothed-out hollow in the earth floor showed where he had lain, moved about, in fact lived for a very long time.

The sight of the animal had a stupefying effect on me; I only half took in the rest of the scene—the filthy shreds of sacking scattered nearby, the bowl of scummy water.

"Look at his back end," Halliday muttered.

I carefully raised the dog from his sitting position and realized that the stench in the place was not entirely due to the piles of excrement. The hindquarters were a welter of pressure sores that had turned gangrenous, and strips of sloughing tissue hung down from them. There were similar sores along the sternum and ribs. The coat, which seemed to be a dull yellow, was matted and caked with dirt.

The inspector spoke again. "I don't think he's ever been out of here. He's only a young dog—about a year old—but I understand he's been in this shed since he was an eight-week-old pup. Somebody out in the lane heard a whimper, or he'd never have been found."

I felt a tightening of the throat and a sudden nausea, which wasn't due to the smell. It was the thought of this patient animal sitting starved and forgotten in the darkness and filth for a year. I looked again at the dog and saw in his eyes only a calm trust. Some dogs would have barked their heads off and soon been discovered, some would have become terrified and vicious, but this was one of the totally undemanding kind, the kind that had complete faith in people and accepted all their actions without complaint. Just an occasional whimper, perhaps, as he sat interminably in the empty blackness that had been his world and at times wondered what it was all about.

"Well, Inspector, I hope you're going to throw the book at whoever's responsible," I said.

Halliday grunted. "Oh, there won't be much done. It's a case of diminished responsibility. The owner's definitely simple. Lives with an aged mother who hardly knows what's going on either. I've seen the fellow, and it seems he threw in a bit of food when he felt like it, and that's about all he did. They'll fine him and stop him keeping an animal in the future, but nothing more than that."

"I see." I reached out and stroked the dog's head, and he immediately responded by resting a paw on my wrist. There was a pathetic dignity about the way he held himself erect, the calm eyes regarding me, friendly and unafraid. "Well, you'll let me know if you want me in court."

"Of course, and thank you for coming along." Halliday hesitated for a moment. "And now I expect you'll want to put this poor thing out of his misery right away."

I continued to run my hand over the head and ears while I thought for a moment. "Yes . . . yes, I suppose so. We'd never find a home for him in this state. It's the kindest thing to do. Anyway, push the door wide open, will you, so that I can get a proper look at him."

In the improved light, I examined him more thoroughly. Perfect teeth, well-proportioned limbs with a fringe of yellow hair. I put my stethoscope on his chest, and as I listened to the slow, strong thudding of the heart, the dog again put his paw on my hand.

I turned to Halliday. "You know, Inspector, inside this bag of bones there's a lovely healthy golden retriever. I wish there was some way of letting him out."

As I spoke, I noticed there was more than one figure in the door opening. A pair of black pebble eyes were peering intently at the big dog from behind the Inspector's broad back. The other spectators had remained in the lane, but Mrs. Donovan's curiosity had been too much for her. I continued conversationally as though I hadn't seen her.

"You know, what this dog needs first of all is a good shampoo to clean up his matted coat."

"Huh?" said Halliday.

"Yes. And then he wants a long course of some really strong condition powders."

"What's that?" The Inspector looked startled.

"There's no doubt about it," I said. "It's the only hope for him, but where are you going to find such things? Really powerful enough, I mean." I sighed and straightened up. "Ah well, I suppose there's nothing else for it. I'd better put him to sleep right away. I'll get the things from my car."

When I got back to the shed, Mrs. Donovan was already inside examining the dog despite the feeble remonstrances of the big man.

"Look!" she said excitedly, pointing to a name roughly scratched on the collar. "His name's Roy." She smiled up at me. "It's a bit like Rex, isn't it, that name?"

"You know, Mrs. Donovan, now you mention it, it is. It's very like Rex, the way it comes off your tongue." I nodded seriously.

She stood silent for a few moments, obviously in the grip of a deep emotion, then she burst out.

"Can I have 'im? I can make him better, I know I can. Please, please let me have 'im!"

"Well, I don't know," I said. "It's really up to the Inspector. You'll have to get his permission."

Halliday looked at her in bewilderment, then he said: "Excuse me, Madam," and drew me to one side. We walked a few yards through the long grass and stopped under a tree.

"Mr. Herriot," he whispered. "I don't know what's going on here, but I can't just pass over an animal in this condition to anybody who has a casual whim. The poor beggar's had one bad break already—I think it's enough. This woman doesn't look a suitable person . . ."

I held up a hand. "Believe me, Inspector, you've nothing to worry about. She's a funny old stick, but she's been sent from heaven today. If anybody in Darrowby can give this dog a new life, it's her."

Halliday still looked doubtful. "But I still don't get it. What was all that about him needing shampoos and condition powders?"

"Oh, never mind about that. I'll tell you some other time. What he needs is lots of good grub, care, and affection, and that's just what he'll get. You can take my word for it."

"All right, you seem very sure." Halliday looked at me for a second or two, then turned and walked over to the little eager figure by the shed.

I had never before been deliberately on the lookout for Mrs. Donovan: she had just cropped up wherever I happened to be, but now I scanned the streets of Darrowby anxiously day by day without sighting her. I didn't like it when Gobber Newhouse got drunk and drove his bicycle determinedly through a barrier into a ten-foot hole where they were laying the new sewer and Mrs. Donovan was not in evidence among the happy crowd who watched the council workmen and two policemen trying to get him out; and when she was nowhere to be seen when they had to fetch the fire engine to the fish and chip shop the night the fat burst into flames, I became seriously worried.

Maybe I should have called round to see how she was getting on with that dog. Certainly I had trimmed off the necrotic tissue and dressed the sores before she took him away, but perhaps he needed something more than that. And yet, at the time I had felt a strong conviction that the main thing was to get him out of there and clean him and feed him and nature would do the rest. And I had a lot of faith in Mrs. Donovan—far more than she had in me—when it came to animal doctoring; it was hard to believe I'd been completely wrong.

It must have been nearly three weeks, and I was on the point of calling at her home, when I noticed her stumping briskly along the far side of the marketplace, peering closely into every shop window exactly as before. The only difference was that she had a big yellow dog on the end of the lead.

I turned the wheel and sent my car bumping over the cobbles till I was abreast of her. When she saw me getting out, she stopped and smiled impishly but didn't speak as I bent over Roy and examined him. He was still a skinny dog, but he looked bright and happy, his wounds were healthy and granulating, and there was not a speck of dirt in his coat or on his skin. I knew then what Mrs. Donovan had been doing all this time; she had been washing and combing and teasing that filthy tangle till she had finally conquered it.

As I straightened up, she seized my wrist in a grip of surprising strength and looked up into my eyes.

"Now Mr. Herriot," she said, "haven't I made a difference to this dog!"

"You've done wonders, Mrs. Donovan," I said. "And you've been at him with that marvelous shampoo of yours, haven't you?"

She giggled and walked away, and from that day I saw the two of them frequently but at a distance, and something like two months went by before I had a chance to talk to her again. She was passing by the surgery as I was coming down the steps, and again she grabbed my wrist.

"Mr. Herriot," she said, just as she had done before, "haven't I made a difference to this dog!"

I looked down at Roy with something akin to awe. He had grown and filled out, and his coat, no longer yellow but a rich gold, lay in luxuriant shining swathes over the well-fleshed ribs and back. A new, brightly studded collar glittered on his neck, and his tail, beautifully fringed, fanned the air gently. He was now a golden retriever in full magnificence. As I stared at him, he reared up, plunked his forepaws on my chest, and looked into my face, and in his eyes I read plainly the same calm affection and trust I had seen back in that black, noisome shed.

"Mrs. Donovan," I said softly, "he's the most beautiful dog in Yorkshire." Then, because I knew she was waiting for it, "It's those wonderful condition powders. Whatever do you put in them?"

"Ah, wouldn't you like to know!" She bridled and smiled up at me coquettishly, and indeed she was nearer being kissed at that moment than for many years.

∾

I suppose you could say that that was the start of Roy's second life. And as the years passed, I often pondered on the beneficent providence, which had decreed that an animal that had spent his first twelve months abandoned and unwanted, staring uncomprehendingly into that unchanging, stinking darkness, should be whisked in a moment into an existence of light and movement and love. Because I don't think any dog had it quite so good as Roy from then on.

His diet changed dramatically from odd bread crusts to best stewing steak and biscuit, meaty bones, and a bowl of warm milk every evening. And he never missed a thing. Garden fetes, school sports, evictions, gymkhanas— he'd be there. I was pleased to note that as time went on, Mrs. Donovan seemed to be clocking up an even greater daily mileage. Her expenditure on shoe leather must have been phenomenal, but of course it was absolute pie for Roy—a busy round in the morning, home for a meal, then straight out again; it was all go.

Mrs. Donovan didn't confine her activities to the town center; there was a big stretch of common land down by the river where there were seats and people used to take their dogs for a gallop, and she liked to get down there fairly regularly to check on the latest developments on the domestic scene. I often saw Roy loping majestically over the grass among the pack of assorted canines, and when he wasn't doing that, he was submitting to being stroked or patted or generally fussed over. He was handsome, and he just liked people; it made him irresistible.

It was common knowledge that his mistress had bought a whole selection of brushes and combs of various sizes with which she had labored over his coat. Some people said she had a little brush for his teeth, too, and it might have been true, but he certainly wouldn't need his nails clipped—his life on the roads would keep them down.

Mrs. Donovan, too, had her reward; she had a faithful companion by her side every hour of the day and night. But there was more to it than that; she had always had the compulsion to help and heal animals, and the

salvation of Roy was the high point of her life—a blazing triumph that never dimmed.

I know the memory of it was always fresh because many years later I was sitting on the sidelines at a cricket match, and I saw the two of them; the old lady glancing keenly around her, Roy gazing placidly out at the field of play, apparently enjoying every ball. At the end of the match, I watched them move away with the dispersing crowd; Roy would have been about twelve then, and heaven only knows how old Mrs. Donovan must have been, but the big golden animal was trotting along effortlessly, and his mistress, a little more bent perhaps and her head rather nearer the ground, was going very well.

When she saw me, she came over, and I felt the familiar tight grip on my wrist.

"Mr. Herriot," she said, and in the dark, probing eyes the pride was still as warm, the triumph still as bursting new as if it had all happened yesterday.

"Mr. Herriot, haven't I made a difference to this dog!"

From the Wild

by

Ted Kerasote

Ted Kerasote's essays on nature, travel, and the environment have appeared in more than fifty periodicals, including *Audubon*, *Outside*, and *National Geographic Traveler*. He's the author of four books, including 2004's *Out There*, which was a winner of the National Outdoor Book Award for literature. His expeditions have taken him to the mountains and rivers of six continents.

This excerpt is from Kerasote's 2007 book *Merle's Door: Lessons from a Freethinking Dog*. Kerasote found Merle, a golden retriever–Lab mix, while on a camping trip. Merle had been living in the wild, and after taking the dog home with him, Kerasote soon realized that Merle could not adjust to living exclusively in the human world. So, he put a door in his house to let Merle live both indoors and run free in the wild.

*H*e came out of the night, appearing suddenly in my headlights, a big, golden dog, panting, his front paws tapping the ground in an anxious little dance. Behind him, tall cottonwoods in their April bloom. Behind the grove, the San Juan River, moving quickly, dark and swollen with spring melt.

It was nearly midnight, and we were looking for a place to throw down our sleeping bags before starting our river trip in the morning. Next to me in the cab of the pickup sat Benj Sinclair, at his feet a midden of road-food wrappers smeared with the scent of corn dogs, onion rings, and burritos. Round-cheeked, Buddha-bellied, thirty-nine years old, Benj had spent his early years in the Peace Corps, in West Africa, and had developed a stomach that could digest anything. Behind him in the jump seat was Kim Reynolds, an Outward Bound instructor from Colorado known for her grace in a kayak and her long braid of brunette hair, which held the faint odor of a healthy, thirty-two-year-old woman who had sweated in the desert and hadn't used deodorant. Like Benj and me, she had eaten a dinner of pizza in Moab, Utah, a hundred miles up the road where we'd met her. Like us, she gave off the scents of garlic, onions, tomato sauce, basil, oregano, and anchovies.

In the car that pulled up next to us were Pam Weiss and Bennett Austin. They had driven from Jackson Hole, Wyoming, to Moab in their own car, helped us rig the raft and shop for supplies, joined us for pizza, and, like us, wore neither perfume nor cologne. Pam was thirty-six, an Olympic ski racer, and Bennett, twenty-five, was trying to keep up with her. They had recently fallen in love and exuded a mixture of endorphins and pheromones.

People almost never describe other people in these terms—noting first their smells—for we're primarily visual creatures and rely on our eyes for information. By contrast, the only really important sense-key for the big, golden dog, doing his little dance in the headlights, was our olfactory signatures, wafting to him as we opened the doors.

It was for this reason—smell—that I think he trotted directly to my door, leaned his head forward cautiously, and sniffed at my bare thigh. What mix of aromas went up his long snout at that very first moment of our meeting? What atavistic memories, what possibilities were triggered in his canine worldview as he untangled the mysteries of my sweat?

The big dog—now appearing reddish in the interior light of the truck and without a collar—took another reflective breath and studied me with excited consideration. Might it have been what I ate, and the subtle residue it left in my pores, that made him so interested in me? It was the only thing

I could see (note my human use of "see" even while describing an olfactory phenomenon) that differentiated me from my friends. Like them, I skied, biked, and climbed, and was single. I had just turned forty-one, a compact man with chestnut hair and bright brown eyes. But when I ate meat, it was that of wild animals, not domestic ones—mostly elk and antelope along with the occasional grouse, duck, goose, and trout mixed in.

Was it their metabolized essence that intrigued him—some whiff of what our Paleolithic ancestors had shared? Smell is our oldest sense. It was the olfactory tissue at the top of our primeval nerve cords that evolved into

our cerebral hemispheres, where thought is lodged. Perhaps the dog—a being who lived by his nose—knew a lot more about our connection than I could possibly imagine.

His deep brown eyes looked at me with luminous appreciation and said, "You need a dog, and I'm it."

Unsettled by his uncanny read of me—I had been looking for a dog for over a year—I gave him a cordial pat and replied, "Good dog."

His tail beat steadily, and he didn't move, his eyes still saying, "You need a dog."

As we got out of the cars and began to unpack our gear, I lost track of him. There was his head, now a tail, there a rufous flank moving among bare legs and sandals.

I threw my pad and bag down on the sand under a cottonwood, slipped into its silky warmth, turned over, and found him digging a nest by my side. Industriously, he scooped out the sand with his front paws, casting it between his hind legs before turning, turning, turning, and settling to face me. In the starlight, I could see one brow go up, the other down.

Of course, "brows" isn't really the correct term, since dogs sweat only through their paws and have no need of brows to keep perspiration out of their eyes, as we do. Yet, certain breeds of dogs have darker hair over their eyes, what might be called "brow markings," and he had them.

The Hidatsa, a Native American tribe of the northern Great Plains, believe that these sorts of dogs, whom they call "Four-Eyes," are especially gentle and have magical powers. Stanley Coren, the astute canine psychologist from the University of British Columbia, has also noted that these "four-eyed" dogs obtained their reputation for psychic powers "because their expressions were easier to read than those of other dogs. The contrasting-colored spots make the movements of the muscles over the eye much more visible."

In the starlight, the dog lying next to me raised one brow while lowering the other, implying curiosity mixed with concern over whether I'd let him stay.

"Night," I said, giving him a pat. Then I closed my eyes.

When I opened them in the morning, he was still curled in his nest, looking directly at me.

"Hey," I said.

Up went one brow, down went the other.

"I am yours," his eyes said.

I let out a breath, unprepared for how his sweet, faintly hound-dog face—going from happiness to concern—left a cut under my heart. I had been looking at litters of Samoyeds, balls of white fur with bright, black, mischievous eyes. The perfect breed for a winter person like myself, I thought. But I couldn't quite make myself bring one home. I had also seriously considered Labrador retrievers, taken by their exuberant personalities and knowing that such a robust, energetic dog could easily share my life in the outdoors as well as be the bird dog I believed I wanted. But no Lab pup had given me that undeniable heart tug that said, "We are a team."

The right brow of the dog lying by me went down as he held my eye. His left brow went up, implying, "You delayed with good reason."

"Maybe," I said, feeling my desire for a pedigree dog giving way. "Maybe," I said once more to the dog whose eyes coasted across mine, returned, and lingered. He did have the looks of a reddish yellow Lab, I thought, at least from certain angles.

At the sound of my voice, he levered his head under my arm and brought his nose close to mine. Surprisingly, he didn't try to lick me in that effusive gesture that many dogs use with someone they perceive as dominant to them, whether it be a person or another dog—a relic, some believe, of young wolves soliciting food from their parents and other adult wolves. The adults, not having hands to carry provisions, bring back meat in their stomachs. The pups lick their mouths, and the adults regurgitate the partly digested meat. Pups who eventually become alphas abandon subordinate licking. Lower-ranking wolves continue to display the behavior to higher-ranking wolves, as do a great many domestic dogs to people. This dog's self-possession gave me pause. Was he not licking me because he considered us peers? Or did my body language—both of us being at the same level—allow him to feel somewhat of an equal? He circumspectly smelled my breath, and I, in turn, smelled his. His smelled sweet.

Whatever he smelled on mine, he liked it. "I am yours," his eyes said again.

Disconcerted by his certainty about me, I got up and moved off. I didn't want to abandon my plans for finding a pup who was only six to eight weeks old and whom I could shape to my liking. The dog read my energy and didn't follow me. Instead, he went to the others, greeting them with a wagging tail and wide laughs of his toothy mouth. "Good morning, good morning, did you sleep well?" he seemed to be saying.

But as I organized my gear, I couldn't keep my eyes from him. Despite his ribs showing, he appeared fit and strong and looked like he had been living outside for quite a while, his hair matted with sprigs of grass and twigs. He was maybe fifty-five pounds, not filled out yet, his fox-colored fur hanging in loose folds, waiting for the adult dog that would be. He had a ridge of darker fur along his spine, short golden plumes on the backs of his legs, and a tuxedo-like bib of raised fur on his chest—just an outline of it—scattered with white flecks. His ears were soft and flannel-like, and they hung slightly below the point of his jaw. His nose was lustrous black, he had equally shiny lips, and his teeth gleamed. His tail was large and powerful.

Every time I looked at him, he seemed to manifest his four-eyed ancestry, shape-shifting before me: now the Lab I wanted; there a Rhodesian Ridgeback, glinting under some faraway Kalahari sun; an instant later he became a long-snouted coydog, born of the redrock desert and brought to life out of these canyons and cacti. When he looked directly at me—one brow up, the other down, his cheeks creased in concern—he certainly appeared to have some hound in him. Obviously, he had belonged to someone, for his testicles were gone and the scar of neutering had completely healed and the hair had grown back.

As I cooked breakfast at one of the picnic tables, he rejoined me, sitting patiently a few feet away while displaying the best of manners as he watched the elk sausage go from my hands to the frying pan. He gave not a single whine, though a tiny tremor went through his body.

When the slices were done, I said, "Would you like some?"

A shiver ran through him once again. His eyes shone, but he didn't move. I broke off a piece and offered it to him. His nose wriggled in delight; he took it delicately from my fingertips and swallowed. His tail broomed the sand, back and forth in appreciation.

"That dog," said the Bureau of Land Management ranger who had come up to us and was checking our river permit as we ate, "has been hanging around here for a couple of days. I think he's abandoned, which is strange because he's beautiful and really friendly."

We all agreed he was.

"Where did he come from?" I asked her.

"He just appeared," she replied.

The dog watched this conversation carefully, looking from the ranger's face to mine.

I picked up a stick, wanting to see how well he could retrieve. The instant I drew back my arm, he cringed pathetically, retreated a few paces, and eyed me warily.

"He can be skittish," the ranger said. "I think someone's beat him."

I flung the stick away from him, toward the moving river. He gave it a cool appraisal, then looked at me, just as cool. "I don't fetch," the look said. "That's for dogs."

"He doesn't fetch," the ranger said.

"So I notice."

She checked our fire pan and our portable toilet—both required by the BLM for boaters floating the San Juan River—while the dog hung around nearby, hopeful but trying to look unobtrusive.

"I'd take that dog if I could," the ranger said, noting my eyes lingering on him. "But we're not allowed to have dogs."

"Maybe we should take him down the river," I heard myself say.

"I would," she said.

When I discussed it with the others, they agreed that we could use a mascot, a river dog, for our trip. Taking a dog on a wilderness excursion is hardly a new idea. In fact, it's a North American tradition. Alexander Mackenzie had a pickup mutt who accompanied him on his landmark first journey across the continent to the Pacific in 1793, via southern Canada. The dog was unnamed in Mackenzie's diary but often mentioned for surviving swims in rapids and killing bison calves. Meriwether Lewis also had a dog on his and William Clark's journey up the Missouri and down the Columbia from 1803 to 1806. The acclaimed Newfoundland Seaman protected camp from grizzlies and caught countless squirrels for the pot, as well as pulling down deer, pronghorn antelope, and geese. Although the expedition ate dozens of other dogs when game became scarce (they were bought from Indians), there was never a question of grilling Seaman. An honored member of the expedition to the end, he may have kept the depression-prone Lewis sane on the arduous journey. Three years after returning to civilization, unable to reintegrate into society, and with no mention of what happened to his dog, Lewis committed suicide. John James Audubon had a Newfie as well, a tireless hiker named Plato, who accompanied him across the countryside and retrieved many of the birds the artist shot for his paintings. Audubon called him "a well-trained and most sagacious animal."

With such august precedents, it would have seemed a shame not to take this handsome, well-behaved dog with us. What harm could come of it? No one raised the issue of what we'd do with him when we pulled out at Clay Hills above Lake Powell in six days. We'd cross that bridge when we came to it. In the meantime, this wasn't the nineteenth century. There'd be no living off the land; we needed to get him some dog food. Benj and I drove into the nearby town of Bluff, Utah, returning with a bag of Purina Dog Chow and a box of Milk Bones.

The only one who wasn't aware that the dog was going with us was, of course, the dog himself. After loading the raft with dry bags and coolers of food, I patted the gunwale and said to him, "Jump in. You're a river dog now." I had been designated to row the raft for the first day while the others paddled kayaks.

Dubiously, he eyed the raft. "No way," his eyes said, "that looks dangerous."

I tried to pet him, but he danced away, making a "ha-ha-ha" noise, half playful, half scared, as he pumped his front paws up and down in that energetic little dance he'd done the previous night as he appeared in our headlights.

"You'll like it," I said. "Shady canyons, great campsites, petroglyphs, swimming every day, Milk Bones, Purina Dog Chow, and"—my voice cajoled—"elk sausage."

I opened my waterproof lunch stuff sack, cut off a piece of the elk summer sausage, and held it out to him. He came closer, leaned his head forward, and snatched it. "Come on, jump in."

He shivered, knowing full well he was being gulled, but letting me pet him nonetheless, torn between wanting to come and his fear of the raft. Carefully, I put my arms around him, under his chest, and lifted. Whining in protest, he struggled. I managed to deposit him in the raft as Benj tried to push us off.

The dog leapt out of the boat, but instead of fleeing he danced up and down the shore, panting frantically, "Ha-ha-ha, ha-ha-ha," which I translated as "I really want to go, but I don't know where we're going, and I don't like the raft, and I'm scared."

I talked to him in a low, soothing tone and got him calmed down enough so I could pet him again. Resting his head on my knee, he gave a huge sigh, like someone who's emotionally wrung out. For a moment, I could sense his many dashed hopes and his fear of people and their gear— not an unreasonable one given how he had cowered when I raised the stick to play fetch.

The others were in their kayaks, ready to go. Carefully, I got my arms around him again, but when I lifted him he struggled mightily, calling out in desperate whining yelps. I put him in the boat, and Benj shoved us off as I held the dog until the current took us. Then I let go of him and started to row. We were only yards from shore. With a leap and a few strokes he could easily return to land. Stay or leave—the choice was his. The dog jumped to the raft's gunwale, put his paws on it, and stared upstream without showing any fear of the moving water. Rather, he watched the retreating shore as if watching his natal continent disappear below the horizon.

His ambivalence filled my mind with questions. Had he been abandoned, or gotten himself lost? In either case, was he waiting faithfully for his human to return? Was his friendliness toward me his way of asking for my

help in finding that person? Had I misread his eyes, seeming to say, "You are the one I've been waiting for"? Was his longing gaze back to shore simply his attachment to a known place—a familiar landscape where he might have been mistreated but which was still home? How many abused souls—dogs and humans alike—have remained in an unloving place because staying was far less terrifying than leaving?

"Easy, easy," I murmured as he began to tremble.

I stroked his head and shoulders. Turning, he looked at me with an expression I shall never forget. It mingled loss, fear of the unknown, and hope.

Of course, some will say that I was being anthropomorphic. Others might point out that I was projecting. But what I was doing—reading his body language—is the stock-in-trade of psychologists as they study their clients. All of us use the same technique as we try to understand the feelings of those around us—friends, family members, and colleagues. There'd be no human intercourse, or it would be enormously impoverished, without our attempting to use our own emotions as templates—as starting points—to map the feelings of others.

But something else was going on between the dog and me. An increasing amount of research on a variety of species—parrots, chimpanzees, prairie dogs, dolphins, wolves, and domestic dogs themselves—has demonstrated that they have the physical and cognitive ability to transmit a rich array of information to others, both within and without their species, sometimes even using grammatical constructions similar to those employed in human languages. Individuals of some of these species can also identify themselves with vocal signatures—in human terms, a name.

These studies have corroborated what I've felt about dogs for a long time—that they're speakers of a foreign language, and, if we pay attention to their vocalizations, ocular and facial expressions, and ever-changing postures, we can translate what they're saying. Sometimes we get the translation spot-on ("I'm hungry"), sometimes we make a reasonable guess ("I'm sad"), and occasionally we have to use a figure of speech to bridge the divide between their culture and our own ("I love you so much, my heart could burst").

Dog owners who hold "conversations" with their dogs will know exactly what I mean. Those who don't—as well as those who find the whole notion of conversing with a dog absurd—may want to consider that humans have shared a longer and more intimate partnership with dogs than with any other domestic animal, starting before civilization existed. In these early times—before speech and writing achieved the ascendancy humans enjoy today—dogs had a greater opportunity to make themselves understood by humans, who were still comfortable communicating outside the boundaries of the spoken and written word.

Charles Darwin, as keen an observer of domestic dogs as he was of Galápagos finches, commented on the relative equality that once existed between dogs and humans, and still exists, if you look for it: "[T]he difference in mind between man and the higher animals, great as it is, certainly is one of degree and not of kind." Darwin went so far as to say that "there is no fundamental difference between man and the higher mammals in their mental faculties," adding that nonhuman animals experience happiness, wonder, shame, pride, curiosity, jealousy, suspicion, gratitude, and magnanimity. "They practice deceit and are revengeful," he asserted, and have "moral qualities," the more important elements of which are "love and the distinct emotion of sympathy." These were breathtaking notions when he set them down in 1871 and remain eye-opening today, even to many who believe that animals can think.

The dog now took his eyes from mine, looked back to the shore, and let out a resigned sigh—I was to learn that he was a great sigher. Stepping down into the raft, he gave our gear a brief inspection and finally let his gaze settle upon the cooler sitting in the bow of the raft, surrounded by dry bags. Padding over to it, he jumped on it and lay down with his back to me. Another sigh escaped him. Within a few moments, however, I could see him watching the bluffs and groves of cottonwoods with growing interest, his head snapping this way and that as he noted the countryside moving while he apparently did not.

"Pretty cool, eh?"

He moved his ears backward, acknowledging my voice without turning his head.

As we entered the first canyon, and its walls blocked out the sky, he took a glance upstream and gave a start—the campground had disappeared. He jerked into a sitting position and stared around apprehensively. Without warning, he pointed his snout to the sky and let out a mournful howl, beginning in a bass register and climbing to a plaintive alto crescendo. From the canyon walls came back his echo: "Aaawooo, Aaawooo, Aaawooo."

Stunned, he cocked his head at the unseen dog who had answered him. Where was the dog hiding? He looked up and down the river and at the high, shadowed cliffs. He seemed never to have heard an echo before. A moment later, he howled again, and again he was surprised to hear his voice rebounding from the cliffs. He looked around uneasily before giving another howl—this time as a test rather than to bemoan his situation. When the echo returned, a look of dawning realization crossed his face. It was remarkable to see the comprehension light his eyes. His lips turned up in a smile, and he howled again, long and drawn out, but without any sadness. Immediately, he cocked his head to listen to his echo. As the canyon walls sent back his voice, he began to lash his tail back and forth with great enthusiasm. He turned around and gave me a look of surprised delight—the very same expression people wear when they hear themselves for the first time.

I leaned forward and put a hand on his chest.

"You are quite the singer," I told him.

Throwing back his head, he laughed a toothy grin.

∾

From that moment on, he never looked back. He sat on the cooler like a sphinx, his head turning to watch the cliffs and side canyons go by. He hiked up to several Anasazi cliff dwellings with us and stood attentively as we examined petroglyphs. On the way back to the river, he'd meander off, disappearing for long minutes, only to reappear as we approached the boats, dashing toward us through the cactus without a glance at the obstacle course he was threading. He seemed about as at home in the desert as a dog could be.

At camp that evening, he supervised our shuttling the gear from raft to higher ground and watched as we began to unpack our dry bags. Then, satisfied we weren't going to leave, he vanished. I caught glimpses of him, exploring a large perimeter around our campsite, poking with his paw at some object of interest, sniffing at bushes, and raising his leg to mark them. When I began to pour his dinner into one of our cooking pots, he soon appeared, having heard the tinkle of kibble on steel. Inhaling his dinner in a few voracious gulps, he looked up at me and wagged his tail. Cocking his head, he raised an eyebrow and clearly added, "Nice appetizer. Now where's the meal?"

I poured him some more, and after he gobbled it he gave me the same look: "Is that all?" Likewise after the next bowl.

"Enough," I told him, crossing my hands and moving them apart the way an umpire makes the signal for "Safe."

His face fell.

"We've got five more days," I explained. "You can't have it all tonight." Stowing his food, I said, "Come on, help me with the latrine."

He followed as I took the large ammo box inland and placed it on a rock bench with a scenic overlook of the river. After lining it with a stout plastic bag, I gave it its inaugural use as the dog sat a half dozen feet off, wagging his tail in appreciation as the aromas wafted toward him. Each day's bag had to be sealed and carried downriver to be disposed of properly at the end of the trip, and we had brought along a can of Comet to sprinkle on the contents so as to reduce the production of odors and methane. This I now did, leaving the can of Comet and the roll of toilet paper by the side of

the ammo box. As I walked back to camp, the big golden dog followed me, his nose aloft, his nostrils dilating.

At dinnertime we sat in a circle around the stoves and pots, and the dog lay on his belly between Benj and me, looking alertly at each of us when we spoke. We were discussing what to call him besides "hey you."

Bennett proposed "Merlin," since the dog seemed to have some magic about him. Benj, who was opening a bottle of wine, wanted something connected to our trip like, for instance, "Merlot." He poured us each a cup and offered some to the dog for a sniff. The dog pulled back his head in alarm and looked at the cup with disdain.

"Not a drinker," Benj commented.

"What about 'Hintza'?" I suggested. "He was the Rhodesian Ridgeback in Laurens van der Post's novel *A Story Like the Wind*. He looks like Hintza."

There were several attempts to call the dog Hintza, all of which elicited a pained expression on his face, as if the vibratory second syllable, "tza," might be causing him auditory distress. "So much for literary heroes," I said.

Someone threw out the name of the river, "San Juan." This brought about universal nays.

The sky turned dusky, the stars came out, the river made its soothing whoosh along the bank below us. We got into our sleeping bags. I watched the still nameless dog pad down to the river, take a drink, then disappear. I don't know how much later it was that I felt his back settle against mine. He was warm and solid, and he gave a great, contented sigh.

He wasn't there in the morning but appeared shortly after I woke. Bounding toward me, he twirled around in excitement, pumping his front paws up and down and panting happily.

I roughed up his neck fur, and he closed his eyes in pleasure, going relaxed and easy under my hands.

We had breakfast and broke camp. Benj, who had been the last to use the latrine, carried it down to the beach. The dog was at his heels.

"I know what we can name him," Benj called out, twisting his face into an expression of disgust, "'Monsieur le Merde.' He ate the shit out of the ammo box."

"Ick," said Kim.

"No," I exclaimed in disbelief, watching the dog to see if he was foaming at the mouth or displaying some other sign of having been poisoned by the Comet. He looked absolutely tip-top, wagging his tail cheerfully.

"Are you sure, Benj?" I asked. "Did you actually see him eat it?"

"No, but it's empty, and who else would have done it? I saw him coming back from the latrine when I walked to it."

"He could have been someplace else." I knelt in the sand and said "come here" to the dog.

He came right up to me, and I leaned close and smelled his mouth. "Yuck!" I exploded, falling backward, as the stench overwhelmed me. "You are a vile dog."

He wagged his tail happily.

"You must be really hungry," I added.

"The question," said Pam, "is who's gonna row with him?"

We decided to draw straws, and Benj lost. "At least," he said, staring at the short straw, "someone on this trip has worse eating habits than me."

We headed downriver, the morning breeze cool, the sun sprinkling the wavelets with glister. As the canyon widened, opening upon a grassy shoreline, the dog sat up smartly on the cooler. A dozen or so head of cattle grazed along the left bank, raising their heads to watch us pass. They were Navajo cattle, the entire left bank of the San Juan River being the northern boundary of the Navajo Nation, which covers a sizeable portion of Utah, Arizona, and New Mexico.

The dog gave them a sharp, excited look, and leapt off the cooler. Flying through the air with his front and back legs extended, he hit the water in a mushroom of spray. His head surfaced, and he began to paddle rapidly to the shore. Scrambling up the rocky bank, he shook himself once, and, as the cows watched in disbelief, he sprinted directly at them. They wheeled and galloped downriver.

Nose and tail extended, he chased after them, his wet coat flashing reddish gold in the sunlight. Through willow and cactus he sprinted, closing the distance with remarkable speed and cutting out the smallest calf with an expert flanking movement. Coming abreast of the calf's hindquarter, he forced it away from the herd and toward the cliffs. It was clear he intended to corner it against the rocks and kill it.

Stunned, we watched in silence. Besides, what could we do? Yell, "Hey, dog, stop!"?

Yet something about his behavior told me that he hadn't totally lost himself to that hardwired state into which dogs disappear when they lock onto fleeing prey. Focused solely on the animal fleeing before them, they can run for miles, losing track of where they or their humans might be.

This dog wasn't doing that. As he coursed alongside the terrified calf, he kept glancing toward the raft and the kayaks, heading downriver to a bend that would take us out of sight. And I could see that he was calculating two mutually exclusive outcomes: the juicy calf and the approaching cliffs where he'd corner it, or the fast-retreating boats and the family he had found.

I saw him glance again at the bend of the river where we'd vanish—and right there I realized that dogs could think abstractly. The calf was as real as real could be, a potential meal right now. The boat people, their Purina Dog Chow, and the affection they shared with him were no more than memories of the past and ideas about the future, or however these English words translate in the mind of a dog.

Instant gratification . . . future benefits. The choices seemed clear. And, mind you, we weren't calling or waving to him. Without a word, we floated silently down the river.

He chose the future. He broke off his chase in midstride, cut right, streaking past the group of startled cows who had gathered in a protective huddle. Reaching the bank, he raced along its rocky apron, trying to gain as much ground on us as he could before having to swim. Faced by willow, he leapt—again legs stretched fore and aft, ears flapping like wings—before belly-crashing into the water. Paddling with determination, he set a course downriver that would intercept our float.

After a long haul—mouth open, breathing hard, eyes riveted upon us—he reached Kim's boat, swam up to her gunwale, and tried to claw his way aboard. She grabbed the loose fur on his back and hauled him onto her spray skirt. He looked suddenly very thin and bedraggled, especially when he turned to gaze wistfully after the cows. He heaved a great sigh of disappointment when the cliffs cut them off from view, then turned to me, floating fifty feet off. Springing from Kim's boat, he swam to mine. I helped him aboard, and he stared into my face with what appeared to be distress.

"You look like you've done that before," I said.

His eyes coasted away from mine.

Sensing his guilt, I tried to praise him. "You're quite the swimmer."

For the first time, he leaned forward and licked my mouth—just once before jumping out of my arms and into the water. The dunking had at least cleared his breath. He swam to the raft, allowing Benj to haul him in. Standing on the cooler, he shook himself vigorously, then reclined in his sphinx position to let the sun dry his fur.

Paddling up to the raft, I heard Benj talking to the dog and calling him "Monsieur le Merde." The dog stared straight ahead, paying no attention to him. Bennett pulled up on the opposite side of the raft. "Merlin, you're a cow killer," he sang out.

The dog flicked his eyes nervously to Bennett, then away.

I had an inspiration. This dog, though a little rough around the edges, was a survivor. He was also proud and dignified in his own quiet way. He reminded me of some cowboys I knew.

"I think we should call him 'Merle'," I said. "That's a good, down-to-earth name."

At my voice, the dog sent me a glance, gauging my intentions. He held my eyes only a second before staring straight ahead. He seemed to know that chasing cattle wasn't going to win him friends. More than likely, he had either paid the price for it or had had a narrow escape. Dogs who chase cattle on Navajo lands are routinely shot. Maybe he had been creased by a bullet, or perhaps someone had given him a second chance, letting him off with a sound beating. That could have been why he had flinched when I raised the stick. The dog now appeared to be waiting stoically for our reprimand, and perhaps that's why he had tried to appease me by licking my mouth.

"Merle," I said in a soft, low voice. "Merle." He gave me another quick look, one brow up, the other down.

"Will that name work for you?"

The dog looked away, downriver, trying to ignore me. Then he began to tremble, not from his cold swim, but in fear.

In central and southern Italy during the 1980s, about 800,000 free-ranging dogs lived around villages, among cattle, sheep, pigs, chickens, deer, boar, hare, other domestic dogs, and wild wolves. To estimate the impact these free-ranging dogs were having on livestock and wildlife, and particularly on the small, endangered wolf population, a team of biologists captured, radio-collared, and then observed one group of dogs in the Velino-Sirente Mountains of Abruzzo. The group consisted of nine adults—four males and five females—to whom forty pups were eventually born, only two surviving into adulthood, a testimony to the many dangers the free-ranging dogs faced as they eked out a livelihood. They were killed by people—primarily herders—as well as by foxes, wolves, and predatory birds.

Contrary to popular belief, the biologists discovered that the dogs didn't prey on wildlife or livestock. Instead, they scavenged at garbage dumps, as did most of the wolves. Since large groups of dogs prevented the smaller packs of wolves from feeding, the wolves sometimes went hungry. The researchers also noted that a small percentage of the dogs hunted deer and other wildlife, their prey varying by locale. In the Galápagos Islands, for instance, free-ranging dogs had been seen to prey on marine iguanas. On occasion, the Italian researchers added, such dogs were known to take down livestock, especially calves.

Among these dogs there were some individuals the researchers described as "stray" and others as "feral." The two are quite distinct. "Stray dogs," the scientists wrote, "maintain social bonds with humans, and when they do not have an obvious owner, they still look for one. Feral dogs live successfully without any contact with humans and their social bonds, if any, are with other dogs." Merle—for the name quickly stuck—was clearly a stray, and his previous experience with people had apparently left him both friendly and wary.

Stepping ashore that evening, he kept a low profile, still trying to gauge our reaction to his cow-chasing incident from a distance. Even when I filled his bowl with kibble, he studied me with caution. I slapped my hip and called, "Come on, chow's on." I rattled the bowl, put it down, clapped my hands, and extended them to his dinner.

His mistrust evaporated in an instant. Bounding forward, he devoured his food. When he was done, he let me rub his flanks. I put my face between his shoulder blades and blew a noisy breath into his fur. This made him wriggle in delight. Then I opened my lunch bag and cut him a piece of elk summer sausage. He plumped his bottom in the sand, whisking his tail back and forth as I handed him the tidbit. He took it from my fingers with care.

I knew that I was probably sending him a

mixed message, since elk and cattle are both red meat. But if he and I stayed together, I reckoned we could sort this out in time.

During the next few days, he rode on the cooler and swam among the kayaks. He slept between us and sat around the stove, as polite and amiable a dog as one could wish for. The river became wilder, losing itself in deep canyons, and no more cattle appeared to tempt him. We also kept the latrine covered. Merle would follow us to it and sit a ways off, his expression turning wistful when the user of the latrine rose and closed its lid.

Once, after we climbed to an overlook high above the river, Benj, who is an avid herpetologist, caught a desert spiny lizard. I had seen Merle chase several jackrabbits—unsuccessfully—but when Benj offered him the ten-inch-long lizard, its tongue flicking in and out, to gauge his reaction, Merle backed up several paces, his eyes filled with worry. "That is a dangerous animal," they seemed to say, which was somewhat true—although desert spiny lizards eat mainly insects, and sometimes other lizards, they have powerful jaws that can inflict a nasty bite. Benj brought the lizard closer to him, but Merle would have nothing of it. He snorted several times, continuing to back up.

"Maybe he got bit by one," Benj said, "or just doesn't like reptiles."

A couple of days later, I saw Merle behave in a way that lent some credence to both of Benj's guesses. As Merle and I walked along a bench above the river, our path joined that of a sidewinder rattlesnake, its trail curving through the sand. Merle took in a noseful of the spoor, lifted his head sharply, and studied the terrain ahead with concern.

"Snake," I said, trying to teach him the English word.

He glanced back at me, only the very tip of his tail moving, acknowledging what I had said. Then he took several steps to the side of the sidewinder's trail and walked parallel to it, keeping his eyes peeled.

On our way back to camp, we passed some coyote scat—two turds, each about four inches long and an inch in diameter. Merle's reaction to them was entirely different. He gave the coyote poop a sniff, then poked at the turds with his right paw, his nails taking them apart. He gave them another deep smell, like a wine connoisseur who has swirled his glass and is appreciating the wine's bouquet. His gaze became excited.

"*Coyoté*," I said, giving the word its Spanish pronunciation.

He wagged his tail hard, cocked his leg, and squirted the coyote turds before enthusiastically scraping his hind legs over them. Puffing himself up, he trotted down the trail with his head swiveling dramatically from side to side, his entire body language announcing, "I will beat the living shit out of you if I find you."

His familiarity with the creatures of the desert impressed me; his burnished golden coat attracted me; his eyes wooed me. Yet for all the time we spent together, and despite sleeping by my side, Merle wasn't overt in his affections. He didn't put his head on anyone's lap; he didn't lick; he didn't offer his paw. Though still a pup, he was reserved and dignified. Life had taught him that trust needed to be earned.

On our last morning, as we came in sight of the muddy beach at Clay Hills and our waiting cars, which a shuttle company had driven down for us, I began to wonder whether this stray dog, with his mixture of fear and equanimity, would stick around or head off into the desert. I had once met a stray dog in Nepal who I had thought was attached to me, but he had fooled me completely.

Like Merle, he simply appeared, walking into our camp in the remote Hunku Valley that lies beneath the great divide on which Mount Everest looms. A young, black-and-brown Tibetan Mastiff, what Tibetans call a *Do Khyi*, he also had good manners and a highly evolved sense of how to feather his nest. He tagged along, eating our food and sleeping pressed to my sleeping bag, as my two companions and I trekked up the valley.

At the head of the valley, as we entered an icefall, the dog (whom we had named simply "the Khyi") went off to the left. Shortly he returned, sending us beseeching looks as he ran off again, trying to get us to follow him. We ignored him, keeping to our path, which we could see from the map was the direct route to the pass we had to climb. Many torturous hours later, we emerged from the icefall, only to find the Khyi, sitting there, waiting for us, an "I told you so" look on his face. Clearly, he had been this way before and knew a shortcut.

The next day we had to climb the Amphu Labtsa, a pass at the head of the valley that is the only way to exit the Hunku without retracing your steps. It's nineteen thousand feet above sea level, and to approach it you have to ascend increasingly steep snowfields, which the Khyi, still at our heels, navigated handily. However, when the last snowfield turned into a gully full of ice bulges, the Khyi was stopped short. We had fixed ropes for our four porters, and I brought up the rear, "jumaring" on the rope (using a mechanical device with teeth to assist in the ascent) and pushing the Khyi ahead of me, boosting him over the ice bulges.

At last, we came to a bulge too long and steep for the Khyi to surmount even with a push from me. He sat, unable to go up or down. Had he attempted to do either, he surely would have slipped and tumbled to his death. Like Merle, he was a four-eyed dog, with two tan patches on his black forehead, directly above his very brown eyes. He was unable to move them independently, as Merle could, yet, when furrowed, they gave him an expression of sobriety and command. Now, they seemed to say, "You know what we have to do."

I took off my pack and opened it wide. Since the ropes and ice-climbing gear were being employed on the mountain, I now had extra room. Lifting the Khyi by his armpits, I slipped him into the pack tail-first. He didn't protest in the least, and I continued up the ropes. He wasn't quite as big as Merle, maybe forty-five pounds. Still, given the other gear I was carrying, it meant I was toting about sixty-five pounds. Occasionally, the load pulled me off my stance, my crampons scraping across the ice as I swung on the rope.

The Khyi didn't stir. When I looked around, he met my eye and gave me a steady look, unfazed by the steep angle. Not once did he lick me.

At the top, we cramponed along the ridge crest, searching for an exit and discovering that we were at an impasse. The only negotiable descent was via a ledge whose far edge connected to a steep snowfield that in turn led to the glacier and valley far below. However, the ledge was about a hundred feet below us, and we couldn't climb down to it, a fact that was brought home to us by one of the porters who, shifting his backpack nervously, dropped his sleeping bag. We watched it grow smaller and smaller as it tumbled several thousand feet through space until it hit the glacier.

The only way down, we could see, was to follow the sleeping bag's fall—a free rappel, with nothing beneath our feet but the dizzying drop. Since my friends had led up, I offered to lead down. When I swung off into space, aiming for the tiny ledge, the Khyi, immobile till then, gave a small whine. Braking myself on the rope, I turned and saw him peering down into the abyss, his eyes enormously wide. He glanced at me and whined again. He did not like the exposure.

When I reached the two-foot-wide ledge, I let him out of the pack, for he had begun to struggle. He ran several feet to the right, where the ledge ended, and a dozen feet to the left, where it merged into the steep snowfield on which it was obvious he'd get no purchase with his claws. He sat down, looking as if the wind had been knocked out of him, and stared to the distant valley. When the others arrived, he came over to me, sat by my pack, and let me put him in it. This was a dog without illusions.

We did two more rappels before the steep angle of the snowfield lessened. I took the Khyi from my pack, and without so much as a backward glance he ran off into the approaching night, his dark form vanishing on the glacier below.

Out of water, almost out of food, we camped in a sandy swale, glad to be down and looking forward to the morning, when we could cross the glacier and moraine in safety. When the sun rose, we found a trickle of ice melt, and as we sat drinking our tea, who should come trotting up but the Khyi. He greeted each person briefly with his plume of waving tail, then came and sat before me. Looking me in the eyes, he raised his paw. I clasped him on the shoulder, and he put his paw on my arm in a comradely gesture. He stared into my eyes for a long moment, then whirled and disappeared among the ice.

I never saw him again, though a good friend of mine met him the next climbing season when the Khyi approached his camp only a few miles from where he had departed from us. He was convivial and well mannered, and he attached himself to my friend's party, accompanying them to Island Peak's 20,300-foot-high summit.

Now, as we floated toward Clay Hills, I watched Merle sitting on the cooler and wondered whether he'd walk off into the desert to await the next group of river runners—like the Khyi, a canine adventurer and opportunist, a professional stray, a dog who liked scenic trips, his luminous eyes having said to how many others, "I am yours . . . for some elk sausage and a free ride."

We de-rigged the raft and loaded it in Benj's truck. We lashed down the kayaks, and Merle watched our every move with attention and without the least inclination to take off. We gathered in a circle, and he looked at us quizzically.

"What should we do with him?" I asked.

Pam had a little Husky named Kira and couldn't take on another dog. Bennett wasn't sure of his future. Benj lived and worked at the Teton Science School, where dogs weren't allowed, and Kim said a dog didn't fit into her lifestyle. I wondered whether a dog really fit into mine, and what I might do with him when I traveled on assignments. When I voiced this concern, Pam and Benj volunteered to dogsit.

Merle stared at me from under his crinkled brows. The thought of leaving him on this riverbank suddenly struck me as one of the great blunders I might make in my life.

"You want to become a Wyoming dog?" I asked him, thinking of how his back had felt against mine in the night and the expression on his face when he had realized that the howls echoing from the canyon walls were his own.

He gave his tail a slow, uncertain swish, having read the somewhat uneasy tenor of our discussion.

Our decision was delayed momentarily as Pam and Bennett, needing to be off, began a round of hugs with us. After they had driven off, Kim

climbed into the truck, as did Benj. I held the door open for Merle. "Let's go. You're a Wyoming dog now—if you want."

A warm, sloppy grin spread across his face: "Me? You mean me?"

"Yep, I mean you," I said gently. "Come on, let's go home."

He bounded in and settled himself behind the front seats on the floor.

An hour later, I turned around and said, "Hey, you guys, how you doing back there?"

Kim gave a thumbs-up, and Merle, who had fallen asleep, opened one eye and gave me a contented thump of his tail.

Just Like Me

by

Mike Lingenfelter and David Frei

After two serious heart attacks and open-heart surgery, Mike Lingenfelter thought his life was over. Suffering from unstable angina, he was constantly at risk of another mild attack, let alone one that could take his life. His life's work as an accomplished engineer was now on the back burner, and he was depressed that he couldn't accomplish even simple tasks by himself. A doctor recommended getting a therapy dog to motivate Mike to get out of the house and exercise. Dakota, a rescued golden retriever with his own laundry list of medical issues, became that dog. In the following excerpt from *The Angel by My Side*, Mike, with the help of David Frei—the cohost of USA Network's annual telecast of the popular Westminster Kennel Club dog show—tells how he first met Dakota and became convinced they were a perfect match.

*H*ow does a dog end up chained to a stake in someone's backyard in the sweltering Texas heat? Did he eat someone's shoe or chew up a feather pillow? Did he have a housebreaking accident on some pricey new carpet? Or did he just become too expensive all of a sudden? What changed him from a happy, loyal, tail-wagging member of the family to an afterthought and a burden?

Personally, I'll never understand it, but that's how Karen Costello found this young golden-red dog one spring day in Houston in 1994. He was skinny and in poor health, and he looked as if he'd been pretty much ignored for some time.

Karen learned about this dog when she received a call from a woman who claimed that the dog wasn't hers, nor did she know to whom it belonged, but she wanted it gone. If Karen didn't come and get it, the caller said, she'd have it put to sleep. This was the classic "rescue story" that Karen and others in her field often heard—people who wouldn't take responsibility for a bad situation suddenly didn't own the dog; in fact, they didn't know who the owner was, but they were just trying to help. Karen had been working in rescue long enough to know that she was often hearing stories that weren't 100-percent factual. She had no way of knowing what was true and what wasn't—but her job was to save the dog, not judge the people.

Rescue didn't automatically mean a happy ending to a sad story. Sometimes dogs can't be rescued, usually for reasons of health or temperament. Karen was concerned that the dog she saw in front of her might be headed toward one of those unhappy endings, and she'd seen enough of those over the years. There were so many dogs out there that could be saved—but she didn't always have the time or the energy, and the club didn't always have the funds to fix everything.

But as Karen approached this dog, she saw something in his personality and in his eyes. She said a little prayer to herself: "Please, God, help me make this one end with smiles everywhere." Symbolically, it was important to Karen to give a rescued dog a new name whenever she could, which indicated a fresh start. She had one ready for this youngster.

"C'mon, Dakota, let's get out of here," she said softly, as she unfastened the chain and gathered him up. *Dakota* was a Native American word for "friend," and the dog now named as such was wagging his tail for her. Karen smiled—for her, rescue was often about small victories.

Karen placed Dakota in a dog crate in the back of her car and headed

off to see her veterinarian. As it turned out, Dakota had heartworm disease, which is spread by mosquitoes. Mosquitoes carry a parasite called *dirofilaria immitis* that lives in the arteries and the heart chambers of dogs. As these parasites multiply, they can create life-threatening blockages in the dog's arteries and heart. Being chained up in a backyard where mosquitoes were abundant—as Dakota had been—would expose a dog to greater risk of becoming infected. Infected dogs can be treated, but the treatment is delicate and can also create fatal blockages, as these worms are killed and carried out of the heart a few at a time.

Karen's veterinarian started the treatment for Dakota right away. Early in the process, however, his heart stopped, probably from a blockage. After some anxious moments, Dakota survived, and the heartworm was eventually

eradicated. He was seemingly on the road back to good health and that happy ending Karen had hoped for.

Because of his personality, the rescue people decided that Dakota would make a good service-dog candidate, so they donated him to the Texas Service and Hearing Dogs organization. Dakota passed all of the required temperament tests and began the program. But after a couple of months of training, a routine x-ray revealed an old injury, which apparently went untreated at the time it occurred. It was impossible to know exactly how it may have happened, but the ball of his femur had been driven through his hipbone. Maybe Dakota had been hit by a car or suffered some other trauma during his puppyhood. The cause didn't really matter, but Dakota ended up failing his physical exam. It was amazing that he almost made it through the entire training program before his broken hip was noticed.

The school sent him back to Karen, and she placed him in a foster home with a club member while the GHGRC (Greater Houston Golden Retriever Club) decided what to do next. Dakota didn't seem to be in any pain, but he still needed to have hip surgery to prevent future suffering and arthritis. It would be an expensive procedure, and the club wasn't able to pay for it.

When Karen spoke to my wife Nancy and me about this dog, she said, "This guy was an x-ray away from being a service dog. Why don't you go visit Dakota at his foster home, and if you think you'd like to get to know him a little better, take him home for the weekend. He's probably very well prepared to be a therapy dog for you—but he does come with a pretty extensive medical file."

That made me smile. "Well, so do I," I told her. "And my heart stopped, too, just like his did." I was surprising myself. It almost sounded as if I was looking for reasons for this to happen.

"I can't make any promises," Karen said. "But if it does work out between you, then you'll need to get him that hip surgery."

That night, Nancy and I drove down to southwest Houston to see Dakota. We took our dog Abbey with us—after all, she was a part of this, too.

Foster homes for rescue dogs can be hard to find, and you never know when people with their hearts in the right place are trying to do more than they really can, either physically or mentally. We were trying not to be judgmental, but we were a little put off by the fact that Dakota was living in a crate in this person's kitchen.

Nancy didn't like that at all, for it seemed as if Dakota was being held, not "homed," as rescue people like to say. "I guess it's better than being at the shelter," she said to me quietly.

Dakota's foster "parent" opened the door of the crate to let him out. At first, he seemed a little subdued and wary of us. This struck us as a bit unusual, since most golden retrievers act like your best friend as soon as they see you.

Dakota glanced around the room and then went directly to Abbey and gave her a little growl. Then he moved to Nancy, and his tail started wagging slowly. He looked at me for about two seconds—he was smart enough to know which of us he had to win over, so he went back to the girls.

He didn't make much of a first impression on me. I didn't particularly like him, and there was just something about him that bugged me. He growled again softly at Abbey, but she kept after him, and soon they were tolerating one another in sort of a kid-like, "This-is-my-toy-and-you-can't-have-it" standoff.

I don't think Nancy was overly nuts about him, but she *did* like him. And it was readily evident that Abbey wasn't going to be an issue. Dakota eventually spent some time working on me, bringing me this green rubber frog he had over and over again. Now that I'd seen him in action, I could understand why he was kept in that crate. I wasn't convinced just yet that Dakota was *the* dog, this therapy dog of destiny that Dr. Attar had in mind for me.

"Let's bring him home," she said. "Let's get him out of here—we could at least give him a break for a couple of nights, anyway." "That really isn't what we're doing here," I said. "We're not here to save him; we're here to see if he's the right dog for us." I didn't receive an answer to my protest, so I reluctantly consented and led him to the car.

The drive home was an adventure. Dakota was totally obnoxious—he spent the trip vying with Abbey for our attention and protecting his green frog from everyone.

"There's no way we're keeping this dog," I told Nancy. "In fact, let's just turn around and take him back right now."

"We'll talk about it in the morning," she said, in the tone that I had come to recognize as meaning that the discussion was over. I think she was feeling sorry for the dog. I was feeling sorry for myself . . . as usual. All of that notwithstanding, one thing was obvious in the confined space of the car— Dakota desperately needed a bath before he could come into our house. So when we got home, even though it was dark out, we gave him a bath in the driveway—just what I wanted to do at ten o'clock at night. That earned Dakota another mark in my "bad dog" column.

We finally got him in the house, and I had to admit that he acted happy to be there. His eyes seemed to light up a bit, and he became more personable that he'd been at his foster home. But that green frog was going to be the death of me—whenever he wanted something, he came over and shoved it in my face. And when he saw all of Abbey's toys, it was suddenly Christmas for golden retrievers. Dakota spent the evening bringing those to me and shoving them in my face, too. I was tired, I wanted to go to sleep, and he was making me nuts.

Nancy seemed to be enjoying the entertainment. He wasn't bothering her as much as he was me. It was as if he was targeting me because he knew he'd already won her over.

But I decided that I simply could not deal with this dog. "This is going to be a pretty short trial period," I told Nancy. "This is the most obnoxious animal I've ever been around." I felt that the chemistry between us just wasn't right. "We're taking him back. I know that he's supposed to keep me occupied and moving around, but this is just ridiculous. He's constantly in my face with that stupid frog."

"Just give him some time to get used to you," Nancy told me. "There doesn't need to be a big rush here." I wasn't buying that. "I can't take it—let's get him out of here. He's going to give me another heart attack."

But Nancy persisted. "This dog has been through a lot, Mike. He's had a bad heart, people have given up on him, and he keeps getting one more chance to survive. Does that sound familiar? He's just like you."

Just like me? Oh, my God. She was right. Dakota *was* just like me—bad heart and all. I looked at him, and I looked at her. "Okay," I said. "I'll give him one more day, but that's it."

∽

The green frog was still on the floor of my living room . . . which meant that his four-legged buddy was around here somewhere, too. When I went to bed the night before, I really didn't want Dakota in my life. But, as I tried to fall asleep, I couldn't shake the last words I'd heard from Nancy: "*He's just like you.*"

Maybe that's the reason Dakota looked a little different to me as I wandered into the kitchen for my morning coffee. He was lying in the middle of the family room, with most of Abbey's toys piled up in front of him. When he saw me, he wagged his tail but didn't move. I tried not to look at him so that I could avoid having that green frog shoved in my face.

Nancy set a cup of coffee down in front of me. "I think he's been waiting for you," she said. "He's been watching the hallway all morning, and even now, his eyes haven't left you."

Uh-oh. Don't look at him, don't look at him, don't look at him. . . . I couldn't help myself. I snuck a peek at him, and he was on me in a split second—how about a little frog with your coffee?

"Good morning, Dakota," I sighed, stroking his ears as he chewed the frog right in my lap.

I'd thought about his heart problems and what he'd been through as I fell asleep the previous night. How about that? Normally I was too busy being angry and feeling sorry for myself to ever think about anyone else's problems. I remembered what Delta Society's website said: *Animals can help individuals with low self-esteem by placing the focus on the animals rather than themselves.* That's exactly what was happening with Dakota and me—I was thinking about him, not myself.

However, I still wasn't convinced that we could make a connection. In fact, part of the reason that I'd even let the situation get this far was because I wanted to get Dr. Attar off my back, to show her that *no* dog was going to be able to help me. I hated to admit that she might have been right . . . but I wasn't ready to return him to his foster home either.

"How's Abbey dealing with him?" I asked Nancy.

"They already love each other," she said. "She brought him every toy of hers that he didn't already have. I think they're setting up boundaries, but there won't be any issues with her if he stays."

I tossed the frog across the room, and Dakota brought it right back to me. His tail hadn't stopped wagging all morning. I looked at Nancy. "Did you talk to Karen yet?" I asked.

"No, but we should probably give her a call and let her know how it's going," she said, with sort of a question mark at the end, as if she wanted to hear my take on it.

Dakota set the frog in my lap and then pushed at me with his nose. I tossed it again, and he brought it back. I was sure that there could be no end to this. He looked me right in the eye, and I looked back. Dogs tend to use their eyes to establish dominance, but Dakota's were inviting . . . and I saw something special in them. I wasn't sure what it was, but I wondered if I might see it again. I thought back to that dog crate in the kitchen where we found him. I looked over at the pile that Dakota had made of Abbey's toys, and then I looked at him.

"How about you?" I asked Nancy. "Are you ready to take care of one more of us?"

Nancy had a startled look on her face—and my words had surprised *me* just as much.

"I've got nothing to do with it," she said, her face breaking into a grin. "You know what Dr. Attar said: Dakota's all yours, buddy." Her look told me that she was helping to make this happen . . . and she was loving every minute of it.

That morning, Dakota and I went for our first walk together. As we roamed through the neighborhood, he looked and sniffed at everything and wagged his tail the entire time. It was pretty quiet out there, and we only went to the end of the block and back. But in that short time, I could easily see that Dakota was very special.

When we got back to the house, I told him, "We're home." Just like that, I had fallen in love with Dakota, and he was here to stay. I called Karen to tell her he was staying, and she told me that she'd absolutely known that the home Dakota needed would be with Nancy and me.

It was pretty simple at first. Dakota figured out right away that if he brought the squeaking green frog over and put it in my face, he was sure to get what he wanted. I got to the point that I didn't even have to see the silly thing—I'd just hear it squeak and I'd grab the leash and head for the door, where Dakota was already waiting. He also used the frog to get me to feed him, to let him out in the backyard, and to get me to pull a toy out from under the couch. He could go from obnoxious to loyal and loving at a moment's notice, and return back to obnoxious just as quickly. He had a good thing going, and here I thought *he* was supposed to be working for *me*.

But to be fair, he did take care of me, too. When I wasn't feeling well, he could tell. He'd climb into bed with me and comfort me, lying quietly beside me for hours at a time. I was still having heart issues (particularly angina attacks), and Dakota would help me work through the pain. He wouldn't let me get upset or angry about anything anymore—he'd come to me, demand my attention, and distract me from whatever was bothering me. This was a great blessing for Nancy, who was the usual target of my anger.

I was seeing the basic concepts of animal-assisted therapy that we'd read about on the Internet. I understood how having Dakota around was helping me relax and take my mind off whatever the moment might have been bringing me, whether it was pain, stress, or depression. I was too busy tending to Dakota to spend any time feeling sorry for myself or thinking about suicide. And much of this therapy consisted of physical activity— throwing the ball or tossing the frog to him, petting him, roughhousing with him, bathing him, or brushing him. All of this was good activity for me.

Even though I had my own four-legged physical therapist (and psychotherapist) at home, I continued to visit Dr. Attar. Yet these sessions were much different than they'd been previously. Instead of focusing on my anger and hopelessness, I talked to her about Dakota and me, how we were getting along, and the things we did together. I found myself looking forward to my visits with Dr. Attar, and I was having fun sharing Dakota with her and everyone else. Dakota was bringing me out of my shell and returning me back to my real self.

Our short walks to the end of the block got longer—pretty soon we were covering the entire neighborhood. People started to look for us. If we missed seeing someone one day, the next day they were waiting for us, wanting to know what happened. Nancy and I took care of Dakota's hip surgery in August, and he and I consequently had to miss several days of our neighborhood walk. Well, we must have told and retold what happened to him a thousand times. And somehow, his rehabilitation became my physical and mental therapy. We continued to meet people, talking to them about Dakota and his role in my life. It was no surprise that I began to talk more about Dakota and less about myself.

My life had definitely changed. Within six months, Dr. Attar took me off of my anxiety medications, and I was fully functional and enjoying my newfound life with "Cody," as I nicknamed him. We were living a life lesson here: When you share your joy, it multiplies; when you share your pain, you cut it in half. As I look back on it now, I was just beginning to realize who had really rescued whom.

A lot of the fun of being with Cody was just watching him be a dog, enjoying how he lived in the here-and-now without fretting over the past or worrying about the future. He was *living* life moment by moment, and he was thankful for every second of it. I loved that about him, and I hoped that I could learn how to be that way, too.

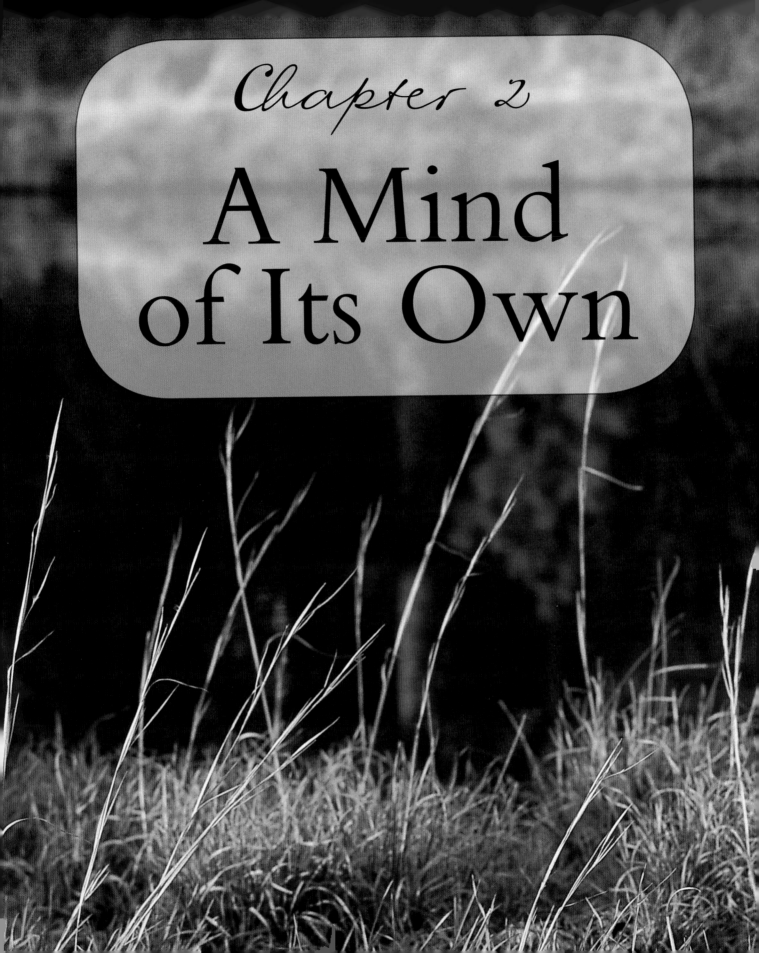

Chapter 2
A Mind of Its Own

The Darkest Evening of the Year

by

Dean Koontz

ean Koontz is a suspense writer of the highest order. His tension-filled stories seem to bring readers to the edge of their seats, anxiously flipping to the next page to see the fates of his characters unfold.

Many of his numerous books feature dogs, including *Dragon Tears*, *Dark Rivers of the Heart*, *Ticktock*, and *Fear Nothing*. *Watchers* was Koontz's first book to feature a canine main character, Einstein, a golden retriever of unusual intelligence. The book is not only the story of a man and his dog, but a thriller and a love story as well, and the book is considered one of Koontz's greatest.

His most recent book (published in December 2007), *The Darkest Evening of the Year*, also tells the tale of a special golden retriever, Nickie, who forms a unique bond with her rescuer, Amy Redwing. Yet through a number of eerie incidents, Amy realizes Nickie might also be *her* rescuer, perhaps fatefully sent as a protector from the dark forces of her past. In this excerpt from the book, Amy begins to realize that she has a special connection with this unusually intuitive dog.

*W*ith breakfast and the morning walk only a couple of hours away, Amy would not let the gang of three panhandle cookies from her. "No fat dogs," she admonished. In the refrigerator she kept a plastic bag of sliced carrots for such moments.

Sitting on the floor with the kids, she gave circles of crisp carrot first to Ethel, then to Fred, then to Nickie. They crunched the treats enthusiastically and licked their chops.

When she had given each of them six pieces, she said, "Enough. We don't want you to have bright orange poop, do we?"

She borrowed a dog bed from the study and put it in a third corner of her bedroom, then filled a second water dish to put beside the first.

By the time Amy changed into pajamas, the dogs appeared to have settled in their separate corners for what remained of the night.

She placed her slippers next to her bed, plumped her pillows, got under the covers—and discovered that Nickie had come to her. The golden had both slippers in her mouth.

This might have been a test of discipline or an invitation to play, although it did not feel like either. Even with a mouthful of footwear, Nickie managed a solemn look, and her gaze was intense.

"You want to bundle?" Amy asked.

At the word *bundle*, the other dogs raised their heads. Most nights, Fred and Ethel slept contentedly in their corners. Occasionally, and not solely during thunderstorms, they preferred to snooze in a pile with Mom.

Even made anxious by thunder, they would not venture into Amy's queen-size bed without permission, which was given with the phrase *Let's bundle.*

Nickie did not know those words, but Fred and Ethel rose from their sheepskin berths in expectation of a formal invitation, ears raised, alert.

Wrung limp by recent events, Amy needed rest; and this would not be the first time that elusive sleep had come to her more easily when she nestled down in the security of the pack.

"Okay, kids," she said. "Let's bundle."

Ethel sprinted three steps, sprang, and Fred followed. On the bed, assessing the comfort of the mattress, the dogs turned, turned, turned, like cogs in a clockworks, then curled, dropped, and settled with sighs of satisfaction.

Remaining bedside with a mouthful of slippers, Nickie stared expectantly at her new master.

"Give," said Amy, and the golden obeyed, relinquishing her prize.

Amy put the slippers on the floor beside the bed.

Nickie picked them up and offered them again.

"You want me to go somewhere?" Amy asked.

The dog's large dark-brown eyes were as expressive as those of any human being. Amy liked many things about the appearance of this breed, but nothing more than their beautiful eyes.

"You don't need to go out. You pottied when we came home."

The beauty of a retriever's eyes is matched by the intelligence so evident in them. Sometimes, as now, dogs seemed intent upon conveying complex thoughts by an exertion of sheer will, striving to compensate for their lack of language with a directness of gaze and concentration.

"Give," she said, and again Nickie obeyed.

Confident that repetition would impress upon the pooch that the slippers belonged where she put them, Amy leaned over the edge of the bed and returned them to the floor.

At once, Nickie snatched them up and offered them again. "If this is a fashion judgment," Amy said, "you're wrong. These are lovely slippers, and I'm not getting rid of them."

Chin on her paws, Ethel watched with interest. Chin on Ethel's head, Fred watched from a higher elevation.

Like children, dogs want discipline and are most secure when they have rules to live by. The happiest dogs are those with gentle masters who quietly but firmly demand respect.

Nevertheless, in dog training as in war, the better part of valor can be discretion.

This time, when Amy took possession of the slippers, she tucked them under her pillows.

Nickie regarded this development with surprise and then grinned, perhaps in triumph.

"Don't think for a second this means I'm going to be on the dog end of the leash." She patted the mattress beside her. "Nickie, up."

Either the retriever understood the command itself or the implication of the gesture. She sprang over Amy and onto the bed.

Fred took his chin off Ethel's head, and Ethel closed her eyes, and as the other kids had done, Nickie wound herself down into a cozy sleeping posture.

All the mounded fur and the sweet faces inspired a smile, and Amy sighed as the dogs had done when they settled for the night.

To ensure that the bungalow remained a hair-free zone, she combed and brushed each dog for thirty minutes every morning, for another ten minutes every evening, and she vacuumed all the floors once a day. Nickie would add to the work load—and be worth every minute of it.

When Amy switched off the lamp, she felt weightless, afloat on a rising sea of sleep, into which she began dreamily to sink.

She was hooked and reeled back by a line cast from the shores of memory: *I have to wear slippers to bed so I won't be walking barefoot through the woods in my dream.*

Amy's eyes opened from darkness to darkness, and for a moment she could not breathe, as if the past were a drowning flood that filled her throat and lungs.

No. The game with the slippers could not have been for the purpose of reminding her of that long-ago conversation about dream-walking in the woods.

This new dog was just a dog, nothing more. In the storms of this world, a way forward can always be found, but there is no way back either to a time of peace or a time of tempest.

To the observant, all dogs have an air of mystery, an inner life deeper than science will concede, but whatever the true nature of their minds or the condition of their souls, they are limited to the wisdom of their kind, and each is shaped by the experiences of its one life.

Nevertheless, the slippers now under her pillow reminded her of another pair of slippers, and the recollected words replayed in her mind: *I have to wear slippers to bed so I won't be walking barefoot through the woods in my dream.*

Ethel had begun to snore softly. Fred was a quiet sleeper except when he dreamed of chasing or of being chased.

The longer Amy lay listening for Nickie's rhythmic breathing, the more she began to suspect that the dog was awake, and not just awake but also watching her in the dark.

Although Amy's weariness did not abate, the possibility of sleep receded from her.

At last, unable to stifle her curiosity any longer, she reached out to where the dog was curled, expecting that her suspicion would not be confirmed, that Nickie would be fully settled.

Instead, in the gloom, her hand found the burly head, which was in fact raised and turned toward her, as if the dog were a sentinel on duty.

Holding its left ear, she gently massaged the tragus with her thumb, while her fingertips rubbed the back of the ear where it met the skull. If anything would cause a dog to purr like a cat, this was it, and Nickie submitted to the attention with palpable pleasure.

After a while, the golden lowered her head, resting her chin on Amy's abdomen.

I have to wear slippers to bed so I won't be walking barefoot through the woods in my dream.

In self-defense, Amy had long ago raised the drawbridge between these memories and her heart, but now they swam across the moat.

If it's just a dream woods, why wouldn't the ground be soft?

It's soft but it's cold.

It's a winter woods, is it?

Uh-huh. Lots of snow.

So *dream yourself a summer woods.*

I like the snow.

Then maybe you should wear boots to bed.

Maybe I should.

And thick woolen socks and long johns.

As Amy's heart began to race, she tried to shut out the voices in her mind. But her heart pounded like a fist on a door: memory demanding an audience.

She petted the furry head resting on her abdomen, and, as defense against memories too terrible to revisit, she instead summoned into mind the many dogs that she had rescued, the abused and abandoned dogs, hundreds over the years. Victims of human indifference, of human cruelty, they had been physically and emotionally broken when they came to her, but so often they had been restored in body and mind, made jubilant again, brought back to golden glory.

She lived for the dogs.

In the dark, she murmured lines from a poem by Robert Frost, which in grim times had sustained her: "'The woods are lovely, dark, and deep. But I have promises to keep. And miles to go before I sleep. And miles to go before I sleep.'"

Head resting on Amy's abdomen, Nickie dozed.

Now Amy Redwing, not this mysterious dog, was the sentinel on duty. Gradually her heart stopped pounding, stopped racing, and all was still and dark and as it should be.

Lady of the
House

by

Roger Welsch

Roger Welsch can best be described as a cross between Erma Bombeck and Dr. Ruth—except he's male and lives in Nebraska with his wife and dogs.

Before turning his talents to writing about canine psychology in his 2004 book *A Life with Dogs*, Welsch was best known as "the fat guy in overalls" on CBS TV's *Sunday Morning*, where he offered up observations on rural and small-town life on the plains. He's also the author of numerous books of fiction, folklore, and humor, including *Forty Acres and a Fool: How to Live in the Country and Still Keep Your Sanity; Love, Sex, and Tractors;* and *Everything I Know about Women I Learned from My Tractor.*

While most of his writing about dogs centers around his beloved Labs, he especially wrote the following piece for this book—reflecting on how the one golden retriever he's owned was one of the smartest, sweetest dogs who ever lived.

*L*ike most men, I can't remember the name of my first girlfriend and just barely recall the name of my first wife. But I can name every dog I've ever owned, and most of the dogs I've simply known. I'd recite the list for you, but I know I wouldn't get through more than a dozen names or so before my lower lip would start to quiver. I'd get something in my eye, my voice would catch, and I'd have to excuse myself to step outside to get some air. The really big trouble for me would come when I'd get to the Big Dogs . . . my black Labs because I do love them so. And if I so much as hesitated when I got to Goldie, the one golden retriever in my life, that would pretty much be the end of my composure because Goldie simply has to be one of the sweetest, smartest dogs who ever lived.

I know what you're thinking: What kind of name for a *golden retriever* is "Goldie"? Well, that's not *my* idea of a good dog name, but it's the way my wife Linda operates. She gives dogs names like Blackie, Whitie, Brownie, and Goldie. My inclinations are more toward Spot or Snowball for a black Lab; or Slump, after a character in a television series from the sixties; or Jonathan Livingstone Beagle, a pop literary reference; or Pooter, after the physiological consequences that dog inflicted on those around her after she once ate leftover corn fritters. Well, Goldie was mostly Linda's dog, so she got to name her, and she named her Goldie.

Goldie was Linda's dog not only because there was a certain bond of feminism between them, but also because they shared a spirit—quiet and yet dominant, peaceful but curiously and incongruously incendiary, shy but without question the undeniable alpha bitch (you should excuse the expression) of their packs. Goldie's reign of power in our household, the Pax Goldiana as it is known in history books, spanned the lifetimes of several of our other dogs, all some manifestation of black Labradors, and a few cats. She was smaller than all of the Labs, but there was never a question about her position as the farm's queen or that this was an autocratic monarchy . . . no democracy for Goldie: What she said went.

Let me give you an example of how it worked around our home when Goldie ran things: Our dogs have been invariably friendly, not a mean one in the lot. But we count on them to let us know when someone comes into our drive or approaches the house. They mostly jump and bark and can appear vaguely threatening if you don't notice the wagging tails or haven't been clued in on the secret password phrase, "Where's your Frisbee?!" But our Labs seem to . . . well . . . lose focus too quickly and too easily. Their priorities seem to shift quickly from "We need to warn the humans of our pack that other humans are here" to something more like "Yea! Yea! Human beings have arrived who may have something to eat, who have new smells to offer, who don't know we intend to jump on them, smear dirt on their clothes, drool on their sleeves, and generally beset them from all sides while they fight their way to the front door!" Or, worse yet, the Labs simply lose interest in the people at the gate (especially if these people actually do pose a threat—you know, escaped convicts, thieves with barber tools, or an insurance salesman) and drift off from the yard gate to investigate a stick, an interesting snowflake, or a dead bird.

That didn't happen while Goldie ruled. Goldie was without doubt the gentlest of all dogs we've ever had join us at our rural Nebraska farm home. In fact, you might say she was timid. She would not approach visitors but preferred to stand off well away from the central arena of canine/human interaction. I am reminded of the old tall tale about the dog that was so lazy he waited until the neighbor's dog barked and then just nodded his head. Goldie spoke from an elevated throne. She did not deign to confront strangers herself. She called on her vassals to do the ugly job of farm security. Yes, she was the first and most insistent to bark when anyone approached our home, but she wasn't as much barking at the *people* coming up to the house as she was instructing her lesser Labrador minions to get off *their* lazy butts and do *their* jobs. She wasn't even looking at the person at the gate; no, she was goading Blackjack, Thud, or Lucky to get up there to the gate and do their assigned job of providing security. "Sic 'em!" she barked. "Don't let them come through that gate, you lazy no-goods! Wake up! Get busy! And don't make me tell you again!"

Then, after Linda or I had come out of the house and okayed this person for entry, Goldie would approach in all wiggly-butt affection and submission, making some feeble excuses for the rude behavior of the other dogs but assuring everyone that *she* had no responsibility for their barbaric incivility. That is, Goldie made it clear that she was, above all, a lady of fine breeding and culture. In fact, she was the only creature in our entire household with papers acknowledging her nobility. These other dumb, loud clunks were only in her service, and she would later see to it that they were suitably chastened for their bad behavior. She never showed the slightest bit of embarrassment or apology for this subterfuge, and the black Labs never managed to figure out that this blond tyrant with her utterly mendacious act was shamelessly using them.

Which is not to say that this unregenerate, regal exploiter was without her tender side. In fact, Goldie was the most gentle, emotional dog I have ever known, even while she was a firm monarch. Occasionally some idiot comes along who asserts that dogs don't dream, can't really think, have none of the emotions common to man, or have no memories. Anyone who says something that dumb has obviously never known a dog, and certainly not one like Goldie. In fact, one of the great mysteries and regrets in my life is never being able to know what it is that someone like Goldie dreams about as she lies on *her* couch (she held title to that piece of furniture in her opinion), twitches, curls her lip, flicks her feet, growls, and flutters her eyelids. Yes, dogs dream.

And dogs have feelings and memories. (I hope I can get through this paragraph without dissolving in tears. I'll keep saying to myself "Rog, you are a grown man. Rog, you are a grown man. Rog. . . .") I have written elsewhere (in my book *A Life with Dogs*) that dogs seem to have a better grasp on the reality of death than we humans do. They seem to understand what death is, when it is approaching, and that it is as much a part of life as any other passage or rite, something we humans like to avoid or forget. Goldie knew that day and that hour when death was coming for her. As we probably should have expected, she approached that gate in the hours before her death . . . a shattering experience for Linda and me . . . with incredible dignity. As always with dear Goldie, she seemed far more concerned with how we were dealing with the imminent event than with her own part in it. And she passed quietly, with the only cries of pain being Linda's and mine.

But even more remarkable to me than that she understood her own passage from life is that she seemed to know the meaning of death, the pain of loss, the emptiness of absence when it happened to others. Three times while she reigned supreme in our household one of her canine compatriots died. One death was in an accident away from the house, and with the others we took care to protect her from what was happening—that is, when we had to have a dog put down to cut short further suffering. And yet, Goldie

knew. Those nights when she had lost one of her pack, she cried. Out loud. (Oh crap, it's not working. Rog, you are a grown man. Rog, you are a grown man.) She never whined or cried otherwise, but those nights when one of the other dogs had died, she knew there was a huge vacant spot in her life, in her pack, in her bed. And she knew who was gone. And probably where he had gone. And she cried, softly but audibly. And it tore Linda and me to shreds. Even while she had worked so hard to comfort *us* during the day, Goldie was feeling her own pain and loss.

Her death came, in fact, within a couple of days of Thud's death, and almost certainly as a result of it. Thud was a big, loveable, good-hearted dummy. As I explained when people asked, "He earned his name with his head." While Goldie had never shown a special attachment for him, she obviously loved him as she loved all of her subjects, and when he died, she went into deep mourning. When Thud died, Goldie was well along in years, and I think she was tired of losing her friends and family. Just tired of it. She was ready to go join them, and so she did. She died with the same dignity with which she had lived.

No, there was not the slightest doubt that she had feelings and emotions. Our cat Hairball loved to curl up and sleep on Goldie . . . let me repeat that . . . *on* Goldie, especially during cold winter nights. Goldie was obviously embarrassed by this betrayal of her canine legacy. You know, "fighting like cats and dogs" and all that. We got the feeling that there was a certain amount of comfort in the arrangement, certainly a shared warmth. And Hairball was a part of Goldie's responsibilities, even if an annoyingly independent one. But you could see it in Goldie's eyes that she wasn't so much chagrined by Hairball sleeping there on her as she was uneasy about us *seeing* Hairball sleeping on her. And maybe even enjoying it—just a little bit anyway.

Goldie astonished us with her mind. She learned and knew things we had never seen before in our dogs, things we didn't teach her. For example, she would take a nap on her back. I'd never seen that before. She would balance on her back, four legs splayed, belly immodestly and in vivid pink exposed for the entire world to see, lips slack, sometimes a tooth or two showing. When I took the dogs down to the river for a walk and a swim, the Labs ran along the sandbars, found something disgusting to roll in, and fetched sticks I would throw out into the deeper currents for them. Not Goldie. She would walk calmly out to just the right depth, in her judgment,

and lie down. In the river. Only her head was showing above the gentle current, and there she lay, quite satisfied with herself, very dignified in her bath, the water running over her and through her flowing hair. And she was one happy dog. The Labs got their feel for flowing water by laboriously fighting their way through it; Goldie figured out how to let the river do the work.

Every other dog we've ever had learned how to signal us somehow that he or she wanted to go out, perhaps standing at the door, bumping us with a nose, standing in front of us and staring, or making some little sound by way of a signal. Not Goldie. With her singular independence of mind and sharp sense for the obvious and logic, she simply learned how to open the door with her nose and let herself out. One evening we were sitting there in our living room watching television when Goldie got up from her

usual roost at the end of the couch and, without so much as a glance our way, opened the door and left, the screen slamming shut behind her. Linda and I sat there open-mouthed, looking at each other in total wonder. Where the hell did Goldie learn how to do *that*? With no trial and error, no tentative experimentation, no thoughtful contemplation, she simply walked over, opened the door, and left. When she came back and we let her in, she also showed no particular interest in our astonishment and admiration. It was as if she were saying "Big deal. I wanted to go out, so I did. What do you think I am . . . stupid? Like the Labs?"

On another occasion I was sure that I sensed Goldie did some thinking and was then unhappy with the consequences. One of her remarkable skills was her ability to detect moles working under the ground in our yard. She would stand stock-still, staring at the ground for the longest time, and then pounce and dig like a madwoman until, triumphant, she trotted back to the house with her nose covered in dirt . . . and a dead or dying mole in her teeth. She then took the rodent to her bed and dismantled it, probably never quite understanding our complete disgust when we found what she had done, thanked her for dealing with a problem, scolded her for the mess in her bed, and then went out to the yard with a shovel to bury the dead mole and fill in the craters she had left from her hunt.

Well, Linda was once putting the dogs out to go to their beds on the porch when she sputtered in disgust, "Rog, Goldie killed a mole or a mouse or something, and it's in her bed. Would you come out and take care of this for me?" Okay, earlier in the evening Goldie had let herself out and gone into the backyard, so it was probably then that she had detected a mole, dug it up and killed it, and carried it to her bed. I got some newspapers and an ash scoop from the fireplace and went out to clean up the mess. And, sure enough, there in her bed was a small, crumpled, wet wad with a thin, stringy tail protruding from it. I scooped the remains up, but something wasn't right about this. The mess was too small, even for a mouse. And it was a peculiar color and texture. And that tail . . . it just was *not* a tail. I inspected the "corpse" more closely and found, to my utter astonishment, it was not a mouse at all but a tea bag.

Linda and I forensically reconstructed the events of the evening. I had fixed myself a cup of tea after supper. I set the expended tea bag on a bit of paper on the table beside my chair. Our guess was that Goldie at some point drifted over to that part of the room and inspected the tea bag. Her conclusion was only logical: "The Big Guy considers this thing on his table to be a delicacy worthy of his palate. He's usually pretty good at judgments like that. And the rule of the house is that any foodstuffs that hit the floor or are clearly abandoned fall into the category of E. D. D. (Eminent Doggie Domain), so whatever the heck this soggy thing on Dad's table is, its ownership now transfers to me, and I intend to snatch and grab and escape with it to my bed before those other bozos sleeping on the couch figure out that I got something good to eat that they didn't get."

And that's what she did. She daintily grabbed that tea bag and quietly let herself out the door to her bed where she could enjoy this wonderful bounty all by herself. Our guess was that once she was safely tucked back into the darkness of her bed, she mouthed the precious morsel. And maybe chewed on it a bit. It sure wasn't a steak tidbit or even the monthly wad of liverwurst with a heartworm pill in it. (That's another thing: our Labs always wolf down the small bit of liverwurst-encased pill without so much as noticing the dry medication in the middle. Not Goldie. She would carefully eat her way around the pill and contemptuously spit the pill out on the dog porch floor where we wouldn't miss it and therefore would be compelled to admire and respect her refusal to be duped into any involuntary medical experimentation. Getting that monthly pill into Goldie was a real challenge for me, and I took it seriously. It was a battle of wits, and Goldie won about as often as I did.)

But to get back to my tea-bag story—Goldie tried tea and found it wanting. As bright as she was, however, while she could get away with purloining the bag off my table, she wasn't smart enough to figure out how to hide the evidence. At least that's what I thought at first. Later I decided that Goldie was way too smart to make a mistake like that and far too proud to let herself be humiliated by being found out. No, that wouldn't have been Goldie. My eventual conclusion was that she had left that tea bag there on her bed on purpose, specifically for us to find and dispose of. She was saying in this that (1) she had exercised her right to abandoned household foodstuffs and (2) she had found our cuisine to be beneath her. She wanted us to know that.

I suppose you can tell by now that even though Goldie has been gone from our family for a good many years, she has never really left us at all. We can't see old photos of her or even speak of her without it bringing tears to our eyes. Smart, wily, beautiful, peculiar, strong. . . . As has always seemed to be the case when we have lost a dog, when Goldie left this earth we were pretty much resigned to the fact that there would never be another dog like her. Do dogs have personalities? Good grief, what a stupid question that is! Dogs not only have personalities, but freed from the constraints of proper society and human neediness, their personalities are stronger and more distinctive than any human being's. In fact, I believe a dog's personality is somehow transcendent—that is, it goes beyond the physical being of that one living creature. While individual dogs are clearly distinct personalities, they seem to be part of a larger living fabric.

As Linda and I have thought about it and talked about it, we have discovered the inescapable truth that while we lament that there will never be another dog like the one we have just lost, every time we have lost a dog and acquired another, the new dog has somehow taken on bits and pieces of the character of the one before so that there is a continuity of the canine members of our family, no one death really being an end to one long, continuing, remarkable personality. I have often joked that whoever invents the Hundred-Year Dog is going to be one rich person and deservedly so, but the real joke is that every dog is a Hundred-Year Dog, since they seem, somehow, to live on well beyond their earthly years—beyond the boundaries of their single minds and personalities.

That is certainly the case with Goldie. Only a part of her passed with her death. Abbie will sleep tonight on the couch on her back, lips slack, a couple teeth showing. Both she and Dunstan will let themselves out the door when they want. Even though neither of them ever met Goldie, they have somehow learned that skill from her spirit still living on the dog porch with them. Abbie kills moles and carries them to her bed; Dunstan filches food from my table, including some things he could have sworn would be delicious but somehow just didn't work out as he had planned and hoped, including one used tea bag; Ab has the mature, thinking qualities that are so Goldie; and Dunstan is undeniably the existentialist Thud.

Linda isn't sure she wants me to tell this last story about Goldie. She thinks some people might consider it to be blasphemous. I think it is a tale of high praise, profound spiritualism, enormous respect, and something no one would appreciate more than a god of mercy and love. Before the turn of the millennium, the Catholic church had a competition for artists to create a new image of a Jesus for the twenty-first century. Linda is a remarkable artist with a skill and depth that inevitably dooms her to obscurity in a field where shallow, political, trendy motives rule. But she did a stunning painting for the contest. Her Jesus shows a power, wisdom, love, and even humor that draw the viewer of the painting into His heart and Linda's work.

I was astonished when I saw it for the first time. I am always shaken by the power of her painting, but this one had something special. The eyes—yes, it was the eyes. Her painting of Jesus had eyes that spoke worlds. It was almost with embarrassment that Linda explained to me that she had had trouble capturing the eyes she wanted with oil paints. She wanted the eyes of her Jesus to be especially full and meaningful. She worked and worked at the eyes, considering many images and models before she settled on these.

I suspect that by now you have already guessed Linda's secret: The secret of the love, mystery, wisdom, and power in the eyes of her Jesus was that the model for those eyes was the soft, warm, brown, loving, deep eyes of our Goldie. I think Jesus would be flattered by the association, and it would make perfect sense to Goldie.

Chapter 3

A Faithful Friend

Pack Maneuvers

by

Arthur Vanderbilt

Arthur Vanderbilt, a lawyer and writer from New Jersey, spent more than forty summers on Cape Cod, half of them with golden retrievers. While his other books, *Fortune's Children: The Fall of the House of Vanderbilt*, and *Treasure Wreck: The Fortunes and Fate of the Pirate Ship Wydah*, tackle more heady topics, *Golden Days: Memories of a Golden Retriever* is just that—a wistful look back at a golden named Amy. Owned by Vanderbilt's parents who retired to life by the beach, Amy loves to take long, meandering walks along the shoreline. In this excerpt from a chapter entitled "Pack Maneuvers," Vanderbilt recounts one such memorable walk, where he and his family are reminded who really is the leader of the pack and reflect on the places Amy never got a chance to explore.

This morning, the colorful sail of a catamaran skims with precision back and forth across the head of the Bay between Round Cove and the Wading Place, right where the *Swan* lay at anchor when Governor Bradford bartered for the twenty-eight hogsheads of corn and beans that would carry the Pilgrims through the winter. And up on the bluff overlooking the Bay, a golfer in lime green trousers and a pink Lecoste alligator shirt lines up his putt. When the golf course was under construction in 1921, excavations for bunker sixteen uncovered beneath a thicket of vines an Indian skeleton. It had not been buried in the usual Indian fashion but rather was found in a crude wooden coffin: Squanto?

From the underbrush at the base of the bluff emerges a bushy tail and rear end, pulling, tugging, an inch gained, two inches, the rustle of leaves, the snapping of twigs, a mighty tug and Amy appears, dragging a large branch,

almost, but not quite, too big around for her mouth to grasp, and twice her size in length, with a network of smaller branches and a cluster of dead leaves clinging to one end, the whole encircled with wisps of dry eelgrass. Here, truly, is something worth the bartering!

At some point on every walk, she seems to pause and say to herself, *Hey, wait a minute: they still think I'm a retriever. I better find something good to bring home with me.* If she happens upon a choice discovery early on the walk, all to the good, she grabs it and proudly carries it all the way back with her. Sunbathers and swimmers who make the mistake of leaving their sandals or, heaven forbid, their socks neatly lined up by the side of their beach blankets, unattended, are certainly asking for trouble, especially if they aren't looking as Amy saunters by with her sweetest expression. Though an empty beer can is almost as good, as is a plank, an artistic piece of driftwood, a small log: treasures all. A real find is one of those rubber thong flip-flops (it makes no difference if it's a righty or lefty), and the rarest and most valuable discovery of all is a heavy rubber work glove a scalloper or quahoger has lost, especially if all the fingers are filled with sand and sticking out, followed in close second place by any glove at all, a surprising number of which she turns up on summer beaches. (It's something about gloves and socks. Fingers by themselves are not a problem; nor are toes. But fingers in gloves or toes in socks are beyond the pale, infuriating, maddening, and the offending glove or sock just has to be removed, yanked off, to reveal those curious hidden human appendages.)

Once Amy nosed around in the beach grass and came out with her mouth shut tight and a suspiciously innocent look in her eye. She has a habit of chewing (and sometimes when they are good and mushy, swallowing) all sorts of bad things—wads of aluminum foil she finds on the beach, tissues she steals from trash baskets, paper napkins snatched from where they fall under the dining room table, pine cones—things that aren't good for her, so spot inspections quite often are in order. On that particular summer's day, we sat next to her and gently, slowly pried open her jaws as she continued to pretend that there was absolutely nothing at all in there and—yes, this can be pretty gross—stuck a finger in, way back in the gizzard area, to see what she was hiding. Out came a wadded clump of paper, which uncrumpled very nicely into three moist dollar bills. Lavish praise from one and all sent her back into the beach grass, returning in a remarkably short time with something else in closed mouth, the same look in her eye. Inspection time,

and the slot machine spewed forth two more soggy dollars. Lyme tick haven or not, we charged into the beach grass to seek our fortune as Amy looked on, perversely refusing to assist us, obviously knowing then what it took four adults scrounging around on hands and knees in the sand a half hour to discover: There were only five one-dollar bills in that particular treasure cache.

If Amy has found nothing suitable by a certain point on a walk, she then begins an earnest search: a rather frantic foraging in the underbrush, testing the heft of stick after stick. But like Goldilocks, she is not easily satisfied. One stick is too puny for any self-respecting retriever; one, about the size of a small tree, is just too big to budge, though she certainly gives it the old college try; none seem just right.

Now, being considerate pack members, we offer to lend a helping hand in assisting her search for the perfect stick. It should be, say, about two feet long, stripped of all bark, solid, clean, the perfect carrying stick. Right? Apparently not.

"Amy," we say, all excited, "here it is!" putting it next to her mouth, a stick any dog would be proud to carry.

Amy glances at it with unconcealed disdain, and as she turns her head away, we can almost hear her mutter to herself, *Well-meaning blatherskites!* Though I would swear there are times when she forgets to add the "well-meaning" and just sneers "blatherskites!" or maybe something even strong in dog language. Like all golden retrievers, Amy is affectionate and affable; but unlike many of her kind, she has moments when she does not always suffer fools gladly.

Clearly we know nothing about the proper selection of sticks. More and more frantically she pushes around in the dry undergrowth where winter storms and erosion of the bluff have deposited a messy storehouse of branches and limbs and driftwood, trying out one, then another, rejecting stick after stick, until finally, like now, she finds just what she's looking for, or at least a reasonable approximation thereof.

"Oh, Amy," my father says as she drags the branch away from under the underbrush, "that's *much* too big. Drop it!"

She drops it, gets a better grip on it, and parades proudly down the beach, tail high, wisps of eelgrass blowing about it in the breeze, the leafy end rasping the sand as she goes, which seems to delight her all the more. The noisier the better. *Oh, I . . . love a parade!*

"Her poor jaw," my mother worries. "She can't carry that. Why does she do it?"

"It's too big for her," my father insists, hurrying to catch up with her. "I'll break off a piece so it's at least manageable."

"I wouldn't do that if I were you," my sister advises, advice I would certainly have seconded had I not wanted to witness the bloody spectacle about to ensue. Just like watching the poor Christians thrown into the arena with the lions, as gory as you know it's going to get, you can't take your eyes off it.

The moment my father touches the end of the branch, and he does know enough not to go for the center, Amy drops it and lunges at the air, snarling and growling and baring her teeth, her hackles bristling. Here is a classic example of miscommunication between the species: My father knows he is helping; and Amy, projecting her dog values onto us, knows that anyone with a bit of sense would want to steal so carefully selected a stick.

"Okay, okay," my father says in disgust, strategically retreating, "see if I care."

"See, I told you," my sister says. "You can't take it away from her. That's hers. That's some kind of treasure."

"But she's going to hurt her jaw," my mother says. "You've got to get it away from her."

"Forget it," my sister wisely counsels.

So on down the beach we march, led by a proud retriever majorette carrying an enormous branch, precisely balanced, the branch see-sawing as she walks so that first one end scrapes the sand, then, as she readjusts, the other end. She couldn't drop it now even if she wants to, which she probably does after a few steps; now it's a matter of pride. She has fought off the surprise attack to steal her stick, and the prize is hers.

We're almost to the dock at the Chatham Yacht Club, our turnaround point. The float at the end of the long dock heaves and falls with the wind waves pushing down the Bay, groaning and complaining as it rubs against

the two metal pilings that hold it in place. The flotilla of Bettlecats off the dock strain at their mooring lines where, a hundred years ago, twenty-five or thirty large catboats anchored, setting sail each morning before sunrise to head out the inlet to the Pollock Rip and Stone Horse Shoals for a day of cod fishing, returning with their catch, to the shanties that once lined this shore.

"Okay, Amy, turn around," my father says when they reach the dock.

Amy turns around to head back.

"Can't we go farther?" my sister objects. "This isn't far enough for her."

"Just up to the rocks," my father says in compromise.

Amy turns to continue on down the beach.

The tide is low, almost dead low, low dreen and about to turn, so the beach is wide. Just above the low-tide line where I'm walking, with our pack leader strutting ahead of us on drier sand, a shallow depression in the sand, maybe a foot across, is filled with water that appears to be bubbling.

"Hey, look, I bet this is a spring," I call to the others, remembering reading about the springs that the Indians had used around this part of the Bay.

"That's not a spring," my sister says with contempt, walking over to look at it. "A spring wouldn't be in the water. That's going to be under water as soon as the tide comes in."

"That's right. That's what we feel when we hit the cold spots when we're swimming. Springs."

"No way."

I scoop out the sand in the depression. As I dig, the water comes to a full boil, bubbling up, ice cold, freezing cold, numbing cold water. The sand feathers out in the boiling ice water and then clears.

"Feel it," I say.

"Yeah, it's cold," my sister admits, begrudgingly, cautiously sticking one finger in and then drying it on her shorts, "but that doesn't mean it's fresh water. That could just be the Bay coming into your stupid hole."

"Let's get the opinion of an independent expert. Hey, Amy, look at this."

"You can't make her drink that. She'll get sick."

"I'm not going to make her drink it. She'll know."

Ahead of us, Amy stops and, like a high-wire artist, turns, her stick swinging her around with it. She drops it, licks her chops, no doubt relieved to find an excuse to spit out her trophy, and wanders over, curious. She looks in the hole with the bubbling water. I wiggle my fingers in it.

"Look, Amy: wa-wa?"

She looks, takes a tentative sip, and then guzzles it up like a college student at a keg party.

"I rest my case."

"I guess it is a spring," my sister concedes. "How'd you know?"

"They're supposed to be all around here."

A little farther down the beach, a trickle of water meanders through the sand above the high-tide line, working its way to one of the tidal pools. We follow it back into the beach grass at the base of the hill to where a tiny flow runs over a shelf of hard clay.

"That? That's not a spring," Marjorie says. "Look, that's just drainage coming down from the clubhouse."

Too late to turn back now. I stick my fingers in it.

"Ice cold! Yes!"

The "boiling springs" of the old Cape Codders. And they've been boiling a long time. On the hilltop above this one, behind a slope, was found one of the deepest shell deposits in the area, the site of an Indian village.

Here we do turn around and head back down the beach. Like Robert Frost's traveler in the yellow wood, we'll keep for another day the beach down to the Wading Place and round to Round Pond. Holding out our arms like sails to catch the wind, we tack to windward, past the yacht club dock, around High Point, and then inland along the sandy path through the beach grass to the freshwater pond.

Years ago, when we first came here and this was all pitch pine woods, the tops of the tallest pines around the pond each held an enormous messy stick nest, a green heron rookery; there must have been easily forty or fifty of them then. And as we walked around the pond, hundreds of redwing blackbirds would raise a racket, darting from their nests in the cattails, then resettling. The heron left for good when the development started, and just a few families of redwing blackbirds protest our arrival today.

In from the Bay, out of the wind, the air is still, fragrant in the sun with wild pink roses climbing through cattails and rushes that border the pond. Are the roses descendants of ones that strayed from around the old hotel? A soggy earthen path, no more than two feet wide, leads us through the swamp on one side of the pond. Overgrown on both sides with cattails that nod over our heads, the air as humid as in a greenhouse, with all sorts of slithering and splashes and kerplunks in the thick vegetation on either side of us as we approach. Snapping turtles? a weasel? a snake? We shiver and hurry on. Not even Amy wants to explore these ominous sounds, and she hurries, double time, straight down the path, looking neither to the right nor to the left as we pass.

On a walk last summer, a great horned owl had been perched, unseen, on a dead branch. It suddenly swooped low, straight at us, its wild yellow eyes glaring, checking to see if any of us—terrified all—might make a tasty supper. Amy never forgets to walk a little closer to us and stare up at that branch as we make our way along the path.

We come out from the shadows and cross the road to the sun-drenched bluff overlooking Crows Pond, the lovely, almost landlocked inlet of the Bay. From the top of the bluff, we watch for a while the tiny white sailboats from Camp Avalon, the girls' sailing camp, tack back and forth. Across the pond the camp's speedboat is idling. A camper treads water at the end of the ski line. "Hit it!" we hear. The outboard roars, the line snaps tight, she's up! She's skimming across the water! She's down! The boat circles on its side back to her.

Off the beach, campers dive from the float and swim between the two docks, their shrieks and screams and laughter rising over the water. In her best dog show style, Amy prances down the beach to the camp's docks, knowing what is there: a gaggle of girls who will smother her with all their love for their pets back home.

"Amy!"

"Amy!"

"Look! It's Amy!"

"Amy!"

"Hi, Amy!"

"Amy! Here! Here!"

"Good dog, good doggy!"

"Oh, she is so beautiful."

"Look at those eyes!"

"I know! Look! You've got the biggest, most beautiful, most brownest eyes, you know that?"

She knows, we tell them, as they kneel around her, hugging and patting her, their hero of the moment.

"Look at her little eyelashes!"

"Oh, look! They're so cute! Look! They're golden!"

"Oh, Amy, look at those eyelashes!"

"Jeepers, creepers, where'd you get those weepers?" a camper sings and jitterbugs.

"What kind of dog is it?"

"She's a golden retriever, stupid," one of the campers answers. "What do you think she is? A schnauzer?"

"My older sister has a golden retriever just like her."

Satisfied at last that she has made their day, and from the campers' delight, her satisfaction seems justified, we head down the beach past the docks where the sand gets pebbly and then rocky under the bluffs, the remnants of the retreating glacier, which also left behind the enormous chunk of ice, stranded like a land iceberg, which melted to form this kettle hole pond. And as we round the bend past the narrow inlet in from the Bay, we hear in the pines on Avalon Hill the crows calling back and forth, awaiting the final "Taps" a few weeks hence when these woods again will be theirs, the campers gone, the cabins boarded shut for the winter, the hulls of the sailboats overturned on the field next to the rec hall.

Suddenly, Amy's amblings from tide line to beach grass to Bay and back into the scrub growth become directed. Her dog radar has honed in

on something ahead. *Dead sand shark! Dead sand shark! Dead sand shark!* must be pinging in her brain as she races straight toward a suspicious lump in the mat of eelgrass down by the water, sniffs it, and then slides right into it with heavenly delight. Up again, and then another divine slide. That's right, get it real good right in there behind the ears where it'll stink for days.

"Amy, that is so gross!"

"Oh, Amy, no! No! Amy, no!"

She looks at us with a dazed expression of satiation, shakes, and then proceeds on, pleased with her new scent.

"Ohhh, gross me out!"

"She stinks!"

"The campers wouldn't even get within a mile of her now."

"You've got to wash her!"

"I'm not touching her. That's disgusting."

"Here. At least get her to go in the water. That should get some of it off."

"Amy, here," my father calls, knowing no one else will do the really dirty work.

With the tips of his fingers, he unbuckles her blue collar, reeking of week-old rotting sand shark. I take a piece of driftwood and throw it out into the inlet.

In she goes to retrieve, as my father rubs her collar in the sand and then rinses it back and forth in the saltwater.

Amy swims in, shakes off, rolls on her back in the sand, pausing for a delicious moment to let the sun warm her belly, then lies down to start chewing her piece of driftwood.

A cautious, four-person sniff test does not result in a single passing grade, so the driftwood is pried from her mouth and into the water it goes again, this time a little farther out, followed by an odiferous retriever who dutifully retrieves it. She shakes, driftwood still in mouth, and then starts on down the beach toward home as if to say, *Enough nonsense; this is pretty expensive perfume and now it's being ruined by all the saltwater.*

One by one we've taken off our windbreakers and tied them around our waists. Here, in the lee of Avalon Hill, there's not a ripple on the water, just the gentle heave of the tide; but out beyond Fox Hill Island, the fishing boats leaving Ryder's Cove hit the swells as they get past the channel markers, and farther out the Bay is rough with whitecaps.

Rounding the beach past Fox Hill, we face the wind again, where on this point of land exposed to all the winds once stood the saltworks. From the old photographs, the windmills, which pumped water up from the Bay to evaporate in long shallow wooden troughs, looked like junior high school science projects, built without any parental assistance, but they did the trick. By the War of 1812, when cannons were dragged in from Boston to protect these operations from the British, Chatham had eighty saltworks around the shores of the Bay, creaking and clacking, pumping away; but by the late nineteenth century, the discovery of salt mines in Syracuse, New York, ended the industry.

Comfortably tired, we wearily trudge the beach heading home, closing our eyes and inhaling the nourishing northwest wind that once turned the arms of the windmills. Feeling like sailors reaching port after a long voyage, we climb the sandy path to the lawn and tumble into the white wooden chairs on top of the bluff:

Home is the sailor, home from the sea,
And the hunter home from the hill.

For a while, we watch shadows of clouds hurry across the lawn, and the catboat pulling at its mooring, and gulls dipping and soaring above the channel. Amy sits under the pines looking toward the Bay, her eyes half shut, then closed, then open again, until she lies down in the shade, dozing and dreaming, listening to the steady sigh of the breeze through the pines and the faraway roar of the surf on the outerbeach.

That was then, Amy. Do you hear it now, in the October wind in the hemlocks outside the front door? In the oak leaves blowing about the lawn?

And all I ask,
And all I ask is a windy day with the white clouds flying . . .

I wish we'd had time to explore some more of the beaches around the Bay, Amy. The whole west shore, you would have liked that. We could have left the car down at a town landing and walked up the beach past the narrows between the headland and Sipson Island and in around Little Pleasant Bay. Hog Island is back in there, with Money Head on one end, where Captain Kidd is said to have buried treasure. Some fisherman in 1946 found a stash of old coins there. Really. It was in the *National Geographic*. And in there around Quanset Pond and Namequoit, that's where the pines are thick right down to the beach, and those salt meadows in toward Meeting House Pond, you'd have liked it in there, too.

But the beach at Scatteree was good, wasn't it? Up around Minister's Point where we would watch the trawlers chugging back to harbor in the late afternoon sun with clouds of gulls around them, calling and calling. Remember that? And the lighthouse beach where the ocean waves come through the inlet and right into shore and you could feel the cool breath of the sea.

There were a lot of great walks, weren't there? The ones along Harding Beach on those smoky days when the southwest wind churned up the Sound and the sandpipers, like mechanical windup toys, scurried ahead of us

where the waves were breaking over each other. Along the beach at Morris Island where the sand was so white and the bay translucent sea-lettuce green and off in the distance you could see the shimmering sands of Monomoy, the Cape Mallebarre of the early explorers. And through the woods of Watchung Reservation right here, don't forget that, that's where we would have gone this morning, over the wooden footbridge across the stream, up the side of the ravine, through the dark forest of tall pine and oak: That was really good wolf country, wasn't it?

But always among our best walks were those closest to home, where the frontier lay just beyond our doorstep.

Traveling
Travis McTavish

by

Kenny Salwey

Kenny Salwey may just be the last river rat to haunt the shores of the
Mississippi River. He cut his teeth on a canoe paddle and seasoned
it with Mississippi mud. He's a hunter, trapper, outdoor guide, self-sufficient
woodsman, and storyteller whose two books, *The Last River Rat* and *Tales of
a River Rat*, have become regional classics. His next one, *The Old-Time River
Rats*, will be published by Voyageur Press in 2009.

Born in the Mississippi River hill country of West Central Wisconsin,
Salwey dreamed from childhood of becoming a river rat. And throughout his
years along the Mississippi, he always had a dog at his side.

In this tale from his upcoming book, Salwey tells of Traveling Travis
McTavish, the golden retriever his wife owned when they were dating.

*J*umping Jehosaphat! Is that a dog or a pony? He ran gleefully around the corn crib, past the milk house, down to the garage, then up the hill to turn tight circles around the base of the old, gnarly box elder tree at the entrance to the garden. His long golden hair rippled in the wind across his huge, powerful body like a flag on a pole.

I was standing in my future wife's farmyard in Jefferson County, Wisconsin, when I asked that question.

Mary Kay turned to me and said, "It's a dog, silly man. His registered name is Traveling Travis McTavish—I call him Travis—and he's a golden retriever. He's my little boy, you know."

Little boy? This dog was a monster! He had to weigh over a hundred pounds, and there wasn't an ounce of fat on him. His ears probably weighed two pounds apiece!

When Travis finally ran off some pent-up energy, he came over to us. I held out my hand for him to sniff, but he was wary and avoided my friendship offering.

Oh, how he loved Mary Kay. She knelt down, and Travis nuzzled head first into her open arms, his big feather duster tail whipping from side to side. She whispered sweet nothings into his ear, and he smiled happily over her shoulder, big tongue hanging out the side of his mouth trying to get at the side of her cheek.

It was the tag end of summer that day in Mary Kay's yard when I first met Travis.

Maybe a week or so later, we loaded Travis and my black Lab, Spider, into the topper-covered back of Mary Kay's pickup truck for a trip to Rome Pond, a short distance from her farmstead. The day was warm, so we thought the dogs would enjoy chasing a few dummies—the retrieving kind—for a good swim.

At Rome Pond the tailgate of the pickup dropped, and a black and a golden streak of fur hit the ground running. There wasn't an idle paw to be seen for the next twenty minutes. The two dogs made their selected rounds to stumps, tall clumps of grass, and other points of interest where they would sniff, pee, and scratch—generally in that order. First one, then the other, over and over again.

Mary Kay and I both wondered, *where do they store all that pee?* Then we noticed the two of them were just going through the motions. It was time to call the meeting to order.

We brought out the orange retrieving dummies. Spider knew all about this game—she had been a field trial dropout. She jumped up and down in eager anticipation. I took hold of the foot-long cord on the dummy, wound up, and gave it a heave as far as I could out into Rome Pond. It landed with a splash, and Spider took a running jump off the bank into the pond, laid her body flat out, and began churning water toward the floating dummy.

Meanwhile, Travis had started for the water when he saw the dummy splash; however, he must have caught a black blur going past him out of the corner of his eye and decided it was too late for him. He now faced Mary Kay as she gave the dummy in her hand a short toss into Rome Pond.

Travis watched the dummy fall, marked where it landed, lumbered off the bank, and made good progress toward it until his feet no longer touched

the bottom of Rome Pond. Now he began to flounder in the water. His front feet cleared the surface of the water and re-entered with the rhythmic sound of *plutch-plutch, plutch-plutch*. His nose was pointed skyward, and his body was entirely submerged. Talk about dog paddle—this was a classic example. His style reminded me of my own prowess in the water! Nevertheless, Travis eventually reached the dummy, took it firmly in his mouth, turned, and plutched his way to the bank. He cleared the water in one mighty lunge, dropped the dummy on the bank, shook himself off, and stood there looking at me, Mary Kay, and Spider. There was a sense of pride and happiness in his posture. His face begged the question, "Did I do good, Mom?"

She assured Travis that he certainly had done good, over and over again. Mary Kay told Spider that she had been a very good girl as well.

For the next hour or so, it was pretty much a nonstop melee of flying dummies, splashing dogs, and shouting praises. Until all four of us, at about the same time, decided we were waterlogged and tired enough to call a halt to this rag-tag game of ours—at least for today.

We retired to a grassy bank under a nearby shade tree. Mary Kay and I laughed with sheer joy like children. Travis and Spider sprawled out in the lush grass and panted steadily.

Mary Kay commented, "You know, Kenny; we're almost as wet as the dogs are. It seems as though they always wait to shake the water from their hair 'til they're right next to a person."

"Yup," I agreed. "It's the darnedest thing, ain't it? Guess it's 'cause they don't wanna appear selfish—hog all that nice cool water to themselves, don't you think?"

She shook her head in disbelief and smiled.

I went to the truck and returned with a small ice cooler full of sandwiches and cold drinks. Oh, how we feasted, two sandwiches apiece, and there wasn't a growl uttered by any one of the four of us.

We were resting further when suddenly Spider sat up and cocked her ears forward and began to stare toward the nearby water. I followed her gaze to see three mallard ducks, two drakes, and a hen, drifting along. Spider began to shiver and turned to look at me. "No you don't, little girl; it ain't hunting time yet," I chuckled.

Travis, meanwhile, also was now sitting up to look at the ducks. However, he showed only a passing interest, no more so than if the ducks had been robins hopping about in a lawn.

After a while, the ducks swam off to another place. Mary Kay and I sat with our backs against the old shade tree and listened to the wind play among its leaves.

The two dogs stretched out nose to nose in the verdant grass and took turns snoring contentedly. A few puffy clouds were chasing the setting sun into the far-off treetops on the western horizon. Several fish broke the surface of the water. From a distant shore, a robin was heralding the coming of dusk. It had been a wonderful afternoon at Rome Pond. No one wanted to move, to break the spell; however, we had to go somewhere that night. We loaded the dogs in the truck, cranked her up, and headed for home.

There was thoughtful silence in the cab for some time. I was trying to think of a way to discuss Travis' swimming "problem" with Mary Kay. If there's one sure way to offend a person, it's to criticize their dog. Especially when it's your sweetheart, and she calls him her "little boy." I was between the proverbial rock and hard place to say the least! I blundered ahead anyway.

"Honey, it sure was a great afternoon spent with our two pals, wasn't it?" I asked.

She smiled, "Oh, it sure was! But did you notice how Travis swims? I hope he gets a better handle on that."

"In time, I'm sure he will," I answered.

Whew, she'd brought it up herself. Now I knew how a fish felt when it was taken off the hook and put back into the water!

In early October, Mary Kay and Travis came to the Whitman Swamp to join Spider and me for a duck hunt. This would be Travis and Mary Kay's first hunt together.

We met up at my Big Lake shack in late afternoon, donned our hunting gear, and followed a two-wheeled dirt road to the south end of Big Lake. Here, Mary Kay and Travis got settled into a makeshift cattail blind. Spider and I backtracked up the lake to an old beaver dam, which was a favorite place for ducks to while away the last hours of daylight.

I began a crouched-over stalk through the high marsh grass, and Spider slow-stepped along behind me. At the edge of the beaver dam, I stopped to look over the top of the grass. Thirty yards in front of me, a small flock of wood ducks and a few teal dabbled in the water. I rose from the grass, the ducks lifted off the water, I swung the gun and shot, and a drake wood duck tumbled. Spider lunged past me to plunge into the water. Before she got to the duck, I heard two gunshots from Mary Kay's direction.

After Spider brought the duck to me, we headed toward our two hunting companions.

We got there in time to see Mary Kay stroking the head of a half golden, half black retriever. The top half of Travis was his normal golden color, the bottom half was plastered with black boot-suckin' Mississippi mud. His mighty tail schlip-schlopped back and forth among the cattails.

"How'd it go?" I asked.

She held up a blue-winged teal. "I got one, and Travis retrieved it for me." She turned back to Travis and said, "Didn't you, little boy?"

"That's great. Good job by all. Let's sit a spell," I said.

We sat on a downed tree trunk near the water with two ducks between us. The dogs took turns smelling each other and sniffing the ducks.

Mary Kay and I smoothed the ducks' feathers, admired their beauty, and thanked them for giving up their lives. We talked of how it was with hunting: happy and sad, good and bad, sweet and sour. This was the way of all things in the great natural circle of life. Gain and loss.

We took the dogs to a nearby spring hole to wash them off and joked about Spider being just as muddy as Travis—only you couldn't see it as well.

Then we walked leisurely back to my Big Lake shack with autumn leaves crunching underfoot like cornflakes. To the rear of the shack, a fire was kindled in the middle of a circle of blackened stones.

We cleaned the ducks and put them in saltwater to soak overnight. A supper was prepared and eaten with all the gusto a day spent in the fresh air will bring.

Later, we sat in front of the fire on an old wooden bench. Travis lay between Mary Kay's feet and the warmth of the fire-circle stones, head resting upon his crossed front feet and snoring softly. Spider lay on her side next to me. Far off in the swamp, a pair of barred owls talked over their nighttime plans from a hunting tree. Now and then, a fire spark would leap toward the stars only to disappear before it got there.

We leaned our heads back to watch our thoughts and dreams, our cares and memories, drift away with the campfire smoke on the homeless nighttime breezes.

Every so often during the rest of that fall, Mary Kay would need to travel due to her work, so Travis would stay with Spider and me in the swamp. By now we had become friends. He stuck by me like glue to one's fingers. He and Spider were more than just friends. Where one was, the other was sure to be. They were like brother and sister.

One day I shot two green-wing teal. They both fell directly in front of where Travis sat on the edge of a pond. Before Spider could get in on the act, Travis had waded out to where the ducks lay. Carefully, he picked the first one up, then waded out another ten yards to get the second one in his mouth as well. He turned, sloshed his way to the bank, and crawled out of the water, holding both ducks firmly. He walked over to where Spider was standing, dropped the ducks at her feet, and looked her square in the eye as if to say, "that's how it's done, little sister. Ain't no use makin' two trips for such little ducks."

He then shook the water from his coat, rolled in the dry marsh grass, brought himself up to his full height, and pranced proudly about on the bank.

In late fall, Mary Kay and I were mighty pleased to each get a nice deer during the season. We rely heavily upon wild game, fish, plants, and such to fill our yearly larder.

The deer were skinned and quartered, and the tenderloins were removed from the rib cages at my Big Lake shack. However, we decided to do the rest of the butchering job at my little cottage in Buffalo City, a few miles to the north. The dogs were put into the back of the topper-covered pickup truck. The venison was then piled carefully on clean plastic and covered with a large cloth for the short drive to the cottage.

When we got there, we both went to the back of the truck and dropped the tailgate. There stood Travis with that "hand in the cookie jar" look on his face. A foot-long chunk of venison tenderloin dangled from the corner of his mouth. He promptly dropped the meat, went to the front of the truck, and sat down innocently beside Spider.

Laughing, Mary Kay said, "What a look on his face, like 'duh, whoops, bad timing, I guess, huh?'"

"Yeah. I was stunned for a second there. He looked like he was smoking a gigantic cigar," I laughed. We both chimed in, "Travis, Travis, what are we ever going to do with you? You big lug."

During the following spring and summer, our little family of four enjoyed a great many walks together. Often we would go to the nearby hill country valleys to follow the cricks. The dogs would find a deep, cool hole where Spider would swim gracefully about while Travis plutched his way across the water. We would all sit down to listen to the murmur and gurgle of the happy waters. The sweet scent of plum blossoms wafted in the breeze. Bird songs filled the air with music.

Then we would saunter through the crickside meadows where the dogs would chase leopard frogs in utter confusion. We admired the beauty of patches of skunk cabbage and marsh marigolds.

In these meadows, the dogs developed their favorite game of "catch me if you can." Spider would jump up and down, give a sharp bark, and take off running as fast as she could with Travis right on her tail. Across the meadow they'd go, through the grasses and wildflowers that danced in the wind—Spider's sleek ebony body taking short and fast strides, occasionally glancing over her shoulder, eyes flashing to see where Travis was. Travis galloped along behind her in great powerful leaps and bounds, ears flopping, his luxurious coat shining in the summer sun like golden kernels of wheat flowing in the breeze. Travis, however, never gained or lost any ground. He seemed to pace himself around sharp corners, zig-zags, and straightaways, always about the same distance behind his quarry until Spider suddenly stopped.

While the distance closed in a second or two, Spider would stand her ground. At once, the dogs were all over each other wrestling, growling, rolling, and playing in the lush meadow grass.

During the course of the game, the human spectators laughed and cheered: "Go Spider, go! He's gonna catch you!" and "Faster Travis. She's getting away from you."

The carefree, leisurely days of summer gave way to the coming of autumn. Mary Kay and Travis went home to the farm in Jefferson County.

Spider and I had much river rat work to do in the swamp. We patched canoes, cut firewood, blazed trails, and made trap stakes. Busy as we were, however, we both sorely missed the other half of the family.

Finally, a letter arrived from Mary Kay telling me she thought something was wrong with Travis. He wasn't eating like he should and seemed to have low energy. She was going to take him to the vet. Would I call her?

The next day I made my way to a phone to make the call. It was good to hear her voice; however, the news was not good. The vet thought Travis had some sort of stomach disorder and had prescribed several daily doses of liquid medicine, plus pills. Mary Kay had to be at work every day in Madison, so she was unable to administer the drugs to Travis.

That afternoon, Spider and I headed south for Jefferson County. In the evening, Mary Kay gave me instructions about the medicines and demonstrated the correct way to give them to Travis. "At eight in the morning, you put one pill in a small ball of hamburger, lay it in the palm of your hand, and present it to Travis like this." Travis swallowed the hamburger ball whole and stood there licking his lips. She continued, "Next you take this plastic syringe with a short rubber nozzle on the end, and you suck exactly three ounces of this yellow liquid out of this bottle. Like that." Travis sat quietly in front of Mary Kay. She reached down, and he opened his mouth slightly as she inserted the little rubber tip and pushed the plunger all in one motion. She then held his mouth shut for a moment to be sure he swallowed the stuff. She said, "Good little boy, Travis."

"See?" She turned to me. "There's nothing to it. It's a piece of cake."

I agreed. "Yup, I don't think I'll have any trouble gettin' the job done for you, honey."

Early the next morning, Mary Kay left for work. At eight o' clock, I took Travis into the kitchen. He sat on the floor in the same spot by the counter as he had the night before. I got a small ball of burger from the fridge, slipped one of his pills into it, stood in front of him, and whispered, "Daddy's gonna be your 'doctor' today."

I placed the burger ball in the palm of my hand, held it out to him, and he promptly gulped it down as his big tail swept back and forth on the floor. Then I removed the cover from the jar, took the syringe, and sucked three ounces of the yellow, gooey medicine. I reached down toward Travis' head. This is when things began to take a sharp turn for the worse.

Instead of opening his mouth slightly, he clenched his teeth as tight as he could. I wrapped my left arm around his head in an effort to insert the tip of the syringe into his mouth. We began to struggle across the floor. I finally saw the rubber tip disappear between his clenched teeth, so I pushed the plunger.

However, before I could hold his mouth shut, he threw all one hundred and ten pounds of his weight into one mighty, open-mouthed shake of his head. It was as if a high-pressure hose had sprung a leak. A yellow spray shot out of both sides of his mouth. Then he did it again, to a lesser degree, and ran off into the living room where I could hear him rolling and rubbing his head on the carpet.

I cannot remember exactly the couple of short phrases I uttered. I am, however, quite sure "Good little boy, Travis" was not one of them.

I stood in the middle of the kitchen, syringe in hand, taking stock of the situation. One burning question kept crossing my mind. How in the world could one dog, with two shakes of his head, spew exactly three ounces of liquid far enough, fast enough, and hard enough to place a yellow speck, daub, or splatter over every square foot of three walls, a ceiling, and a floor of a medium-sized kitchen? It was a feat of gigantic proportions!

After I entered the living room, I realized Travis's feat was even greater than I had thought. There were enough yellow stains smeared into the carpet to suggest he had completed the kitchen job with less than exactly three ounces of yellow, sticky goo. Even with that considered, I still did not feel like telling him he was a "good little boy."

During the course of the day, a great many cleaning tools were brought into play: mops, scrapers, a putty knife, fine sandpaper, a step stool, a stepladder, and an assortment of spray bottles, cans, and compounds. By evening, I had filled several water buckets with tattered sponges, soiled paper towels, and dirty rags.

As I went about my "house cleaning," a couple of other phrases ran through my mind a time or two like: "There's nothing to it," "It's a piece of cake," and "Yup, I don't think I'll have any trouble gettin' the job done for you, honey."

A glance at the clock. A quick check of the kitchen. Everything seemed okay. Mere minutes later, Mary Kay came up the steps to the front porch where Spider, Travis, and I were waiting. After hugs and kisses all around, Mary Kay asked, "Well, how did the medicine dispensing go?"

"Oh, I got the job done all right," I fibbed.

Mary Kay reached down to rub Travis behind his ears and murmured, "Was Daddy a good doctor, little boy?"

I cleared my throat. "Let's go in and rustle up some supper." As we walked through the kitchen door, she said, "My, but it smells so fresh and clean in here. You cleaned up the house. Thank you, honey."

"You're welcome. I just felt I should tidy up a bit." I began setting the table.

It seemed quiet in the kitchen. I looked up to see Mary Kay rubbing something off the stove.

"What are all these yellow specks?" She put her fingers to her nose. "Why, it smells like Travis' medicine. What on earth went on here today?" She stared at me. I knew I had that "deer in the headlights" look on my face—rats of the river kind, foiled again!

There was only one thing to do at the time, throw myself at her mercy. I began to blame my little "mishap" on the fact that I possessed all the manual dexterity of a cub bear wearing boxing gloves. Then I babbled on about how bad it really was and how much better the kitchen looked now.

She held up her hands, smiled, and kissed me on the cheek. "Oh, you big monkey. You're like an overgrown kid. Now come on and tell me how it all happened." We sat down on the couch with the two dogs, and I proceeded to fill her in on the entire "event."

That evening laughter rang through the high-ceilinged rooms of the old farmhouse.

As the days of autumn drifted by, I mastered the task of doctoring Travis. However, the medication seemed to be doing little good. The big guy had little or no appetite. At times on our walks in the tree-studded pasture south of the barn, Spider would try to strike up a game of "catch me if you can." Travis would begin the chase only to turn back to us and walk quietly behind us. Once in a while, we would pat him on his side, and he would wince with pain.

One evening we decided to take Travis to another vet. We could stand it no longer. Something had to be done.

The next morning, we loaded the dogs in the truck and went north to Winona, Minnesota. Dr. Dennis Dammen had his office there. He had treated my swamp dogs for over thirty years, and I had full confidence in him.

We led Travis into the waiting room a little past noon. Doc was about to leave for lunch. We shook hands, and I introduced him to Mary Kay and Travis. Then we explained about Travis' medical troubles. Doc said, "Let's have a look at this big fella. He sure is a beautiful dog."

Mary Kay held Travis by the collar while Doc slowly ran his hands over Travis's sides. Then Doc straddled Travis's back and firmly raised up on his belly and poked and kneaded every square inch of his underside. He rubbed Travis' back and petted him.

Doc finally straightened up to look at us. "I'll tell you straight out I don't like what I felt. There's a tumor, a mass, in there, and it's pretty big. Two things can be done. We can leave the thing as is; however, that will mean more agony and certain death, or we can operate as soon as possible. Maybe I can remove the tumor, and he will recover."

We told Doc we would talk it over and let him know soon. We took Travis out to the truck. He needed our help to climb into the back and whined when he did.

Mary Kay looked at me. "I just can't stand to see him suffer like this. I think we should try the operation."

I nodded in agreement, and we went back inside to make the appointment for nine the following morning. On the way home to our cottage at Buffalo City, we decided to walk into the Big Lake shack.

The late October sun felt warm as it dappled the two-wheel dirt road all four of us were following. The sky was a deep azure framed by the colored leaves of autumn. As the road wound its way through the high ground woods along the swamp, the dogs often stopped to "read" the signs left by the passing parade of critters who lived there. However, there was no spring to Travis' step, nor to ours or Spider's. She seemed to sense that all was not right with our little family.

The sun was preparing for bed when we reached the old beaver dam on the south end of Big Lake. We sat in the dry marsh grass on the bank. Only the raucous cry of a great blue heron and the whisper of duck wings broke the silence. A few wood ducks came in low and landed with a swish in front of us. Spider sat erect, ears perked, nose twitching. Travis lay between Mary Kay and me on his belly, head resting on his front paws, eyes closed. We each put a hand on his back and stroked him softly. Time waits for no one.

In the gathering darkness, we made our way back to the truck.

At nine the next morning, we were in Doc Dammens's office. We stayed with Travis while Doc and his nurse Deb prepared him for surgery. We petted him and scratched his ears until he was put under anesthesia.

In the waiting room, we did the usual. Drank coffee, read magazines, and fidgeted about. I've always thought one could call such places "weighting rooms." It feels as if great weights are heaped upon one's shoulders and chest.

Finally, Doc appeared. His face was solemn. He took a seat next to us and slowly began. "It does not look good. In over thirty years of practice, I have never seen a tumor of this size. It's massive. It is entwined in his intestines and is attached to some organs. I could try to remove it, but I don't think he will survive."

After a long silence, Mary Kay and I said, "We can't make him suffer any more."

We thanked Doc for his efforts and left the office carrying Travis' collar and leash. The tailgate of the truck was opened so Spider could come out on it, and there the three of us sat in a tearful huddle for a long time. At last we told Spider that Travis wasn't going home with us, patted her on the head,

closed the tailgate, and started for home. We drove in silence for some time until, with tearstained cheeks, we were finally able to speak.

"He was only five and a half years old. Travis was the most beautiful dog I have ever known. He had a kind, innocent, unflappable spirit," Mary Kay said. "He had a heart of gold."

"I guess that's why they're called golden retrievers," I answered.

She nodded her head, and we drove on.

Now Wait a Minute, Chester

by

Eric Saperston

More than fifteen years ago, after graduating from college, Eric Saperston headed out on a cross-country road trip with his golden retriever, Jack. At first his goals were just to follow the Grateful Dead and work a ski season in Aspen, but the trip morphed into a documentary film project. After four years of traveling and three years in development, Eric's film, *The Journey*, premiered in 2001, showcasing interviews with some of the nation's most successful CEOs, entertainment icons, spiritual gurus, artists, and global leaders about their tips for success, happiness, and fulfillment. *The Journey* ended up winning four film festival awards—at the South by Southwest Film and Music Festival, the Atlanta Film Festival, the Phoenix Film Festival, and the Lake Havasu Film Festival—and receiving media coverage in *The New York Times*, *Washington Post*, and *National Geographic Traveler* magazine.

In this essay, written specifically for this book, Eric (now a full-fledged filmmaker and inspirational speaker) shares about going on this great adventure with his golden, Jack, whose companionship meant so much out on the road.

*I*nstead of looking for a "real" job after college graduation, I set out to be this "road dog," traveling across America. But since I had never taken an adventure of this magnitude before, I figured I'd bring along an expert.

My golden retriever was an abandoned puppy who found his way to me. Back in college, my fraternity big brother discovered him walking down the street without a collar. We put up signs trying to find his original owner, but nobody came.

Since big brother had just helped me to get elected as our fraternity chapter president, he decided to give me the dog as a legacy gift to remember him and my fraternity experience forever. I was captivated by his thoughtfulness and generosity. Having been raised with dogs my whole life, I felt an immediate kinship with my newfound, happy-go-lucky friend.

Since the puppy had no collar, it also had no name. I wrote down all kinds of possibilities in my journal: Marley, Atlas, Buster, Sam.

One of my favorites was Stay. I just thought it would be silly to have my dog in a park crowded with people and yell at the top of my lungs, "Come here, Stay! Stay, come here!!" Nobody thinks that's as funny as I do.

After calling the dog by each of the names I'd written down, I would look over at his expression, but he didn't seem to react to any of them.

I decided to grab my surfboard, throw the dog in the car, and go surfing for a few hours to clear my head. As the two of us drove down the road, with me at the wheel and my nameless dog riding shotgun, a song by the rock group The Band magically appeared on the radio. The song was called "The Weight," and as its lyrics traveled through the airways and danced their way into the vehicle, the song inspired us both. It was as if a musical Frisbee had been thrown out, which my dog and I both enthusiastically jumped up out of our seats to catch.

> *Crazy Chester followed me and caught me in the fog.*
> *He said, "I will fix your rack if you take Jack my dog."*
> *I said, "Now wait a minute, Chester, I'm a peaceful man."*
> *He said, "That's ok boy, won't you just feed him when you can."*

I immediately looked over at my traveling companion and said, "Jack?" I swear my dog's eyes smiled, and then the little nuthead looked at me and winked. From that day on, he would be forever known as "Jack My Dog."

Jack and I ventured out on our road trip in a 1971 Volkswagen camper bus after college. Our original plan was to follow the Grateful Dead and work a ski season in Aspen.

Challenged by a mentor who suggested I could make the trip more meaningful, I decided that when I wasn't following the Grateful Dead and working the ski season in Aspen, I'd call up the most powerful people in the world and take them out for a cup of coffee. I wanted to learn from them, the values they've lived by, the struggles they've endured, and see what advice and counsel they would give to me and others to better prepare ourselves for the road ahead.

Together, Jack and I traveled across America for nearly four years interviewing presidents, poets, authors, artists, and CEOs. In the process, we picked up three other travelers. What a long strange trip it was.

Our team crossed countless state lines, drank hundreds of lattes, and interviewed over two hundred of the most passionate and successful thinkers, leaders, doers, and dreamers in the world. We endured four rebuilt engines, at least twenty-two parking tickets, and one potentially devastating rear-end collision. We were kicked out of at least two hotels . . . that I can remember.

Yes, we were like the Bad News Bears trying to make a film. We had only one camera, and while on the road, we had to buy the book to learn how to use it. To capture sound from our interview guests, we could not afford a professional recording device, so we did what we could with what we had. We went to Home Depot and bought a twelve-dollar light bulb changer, a fifty-dollar microphone, and two rolls of duct tape. We "MacGyvered" a journey-sanctified, makeshift, sound-operating boom pole.

We funded our dream and our trip by pulling our Volkswagen camper bus into rest areas or truck stops, throwing down a Mexican blanket, and putting Jack on it to attract people's attention. On the stereo, we'd jam some groovy tunes, open the sliding bus door, flip up the side table, pull out my green two-burner Coleman camping stove, and sell "sexy, kind, grilled cheese sandwiches made with love" for one dollar.

Folks would walk up to us, tilt and cock their head, confused, just like a dog does when it hears a strange sound. Then I'd share with them this quote: "To know the road ahead, ask those coming back." Because of that, I had decided to take a year off, follow the Grateful Dead, work a ski season in Aspen, and call up some of the most powerful people in the world and take them out for a cup of coffee. Then I would tell them I was funding my adventure by selling "sexy, kind, grilled cheese sandwiches made with love for one dollar." Then I would ask them, "How many sandwiches would you like?"

Guess what? People actually bought my sandwiches! When they discovered what we were doing, not only did they give me a dollar, but many gave two dollars, ten dollars, and twenty dollars. One time I even got a fifty-dollar bill for two pieces of bread and some cheese!

Now that's what a college education is all about— learning how to market fifty-dollar grilled cheese sandwiches!

All in all, one shaggy dog and four dreamers successfully covered thousands of miles and captured five hundred hours of footage. In the end, we received a development deal from Walt Disney Studios and turned our travel and adventures into an award-winning feature film, *The Journey*, which won four major film festivals.

Reflecting upon an old Chinese proverb that says, "When you drink the water, remember who dug the well," I realize the journey would not have been possible if it weren't for the love and companionship of my dog Jack.

I still have fond memories of driving the bus and looking over and seeing Jack sitting upright with half his head out the window, happily face surfing the breeze with his tongue flapping and dangling in the wind.

Jack only met friends, and he inspired love and kindness in all who had the good fortune to brush past his tail.

When it came to my dog, we had a saying on the road: "From Jack, all good things come." He was the glue and the life force that supported me through the making of my first film.

Family, friends, and business associates alike would often say it was Jack they loved and me they tolerated.

After fourteen and half years of traveling down life's road together and blissfully enjoying each other's company, Jack was diagnosed with cancer of the spleen. The doctor said that he was bleeding internally. If I kept Jack alive, he would only suffer. So I agreed to put him to sleep. I hated to do it, but the doctor said it was the most humane thing I could do.

The hospital room was cold and sterile. They put him on the table, and I looked into his big, brown eyes as they held his paw and shaved a section of

it. The doctor took the needle and administered the serum. I was crying, and just before Jack closed his eyes forever, the last thing he did was put his nose next to mine and licked my tears. Then his eyes closed, and his head gently fell into my arms.

How's that for a final act of heroism? There I was bawling my eyes out and feeling so guilty, and the last thing he did before he died was lick the tears off my face. How's that for a sincere thank you and a loving goodbye from man's best friend?

His passing was quick and painless. Hours before his death, he was surrounded by family and friends taking photos, getting their last kisses, and seeing his unforgettable smile and his tail wag once more.

Afterwards, I threw a party in his honor at one of the best steak houses in the city where stories were told about him, our journey, and the times we shared together. Jack was a magical creature, an old soul who brought people together in joy and celebration.

He was buried in a sacred and special place, by me and a cadre of my closest buddies. The ritual was heartfelt, and the grieving that took place cathartic.

Jack showed us all that optimism, combined with a tenacious spirit and unconditional love, can brighten up even the darkest of days. Even more so, a gentle lick, the rub of a cold-wet nose, or one of Jack's undeniable winks could leave you in awe of one of life's simple truths: Give love and love never leaves you.

Dog
Years

by

Mark Doty

New York City–based poet and memoirist Mark Doty is the author of ten books, which have won a number of accolades, including a National Book Critics Circle Award, the *Los Angeles Times* Book Prize, a Lila Wallace–Reader's Digest Award, and the T. S. Eliot Prize. In his book *Dog Years* (released in 2007), he shares the story of deciding to adopt a dog as a companion for his dying partner. Of course, he just can't resist picking a malnourished golden retriever in need of loving care. Beau joins Arden, a black Lab retriever, as part of the family, and both provide incredible solace in the darkest of days. In this excerpt from the book, Doty recounts his fateful trip to the animal shelter, where Beau and his thumping tail win over his heart.

I was walking down the single aisle of cages—dogs coming up to greet me, barking a bit, or holding back, eyeing me to see what I was up to, all manner of sizes and colors, ears and tails—when I came to a pen in the middle of the room, where a very skinny and very calm golden retriever sat sphinxlike on all fours, serenely looking up at me. He eyed me and began to thump his blond tail on the concrete floor—a gesture I couldn't know I'd come to love, a greeting and declaration that could be prompted simply by looking at him and beaming the psychic equivalent of "Hey you" in his direction. That thump always seemed to me the physical version of a laugh, a little goofy, a bit dumb, entirely delighted.

But who was he? If he was a golden, he was the skinniest one I'd ever seen, a very narrow head, and his chest so thin that the bone at the center stuck out sharply, the prow of a slender blond boat, and his waist was even narrower. The label on the cage read: BEAUCEPHUS, PART SALUKI? MIX, THREE YEARS OLD, TOO MUCH FOR OWNER.

Awful name.

Saluki? An extremely narrow North African breed, something like an elegant, ethereal cross between a greyhound and a delicate yellow rat.

Three? Too much? Well, if he was full grown, he was a gangly fellow, all sharp bony edges, and if this was too much, I couldn't imagine what calm would look like. I knelt down, and he rose and walked to the cage door, bringing his face near to mine, then he unrolled a long tongue, splashed with purple spots as though he'd been eating blackberries. He lay down again and gazed at me with what I can only describe as an absolute openness, as if each new thing that came into his attention were greeted with the same cheerful equanimity, a curious and cheerful regard. He extended a paw in my direction. My body—heart? impulsive head?—said *Yes.*

What on earth was I doing in the animal shelter, thinking of adopting a dog at a time like this? I hadn't planned it this way. We'd heard through a mutual friend about some fellows in the city who were dealing with some of the same crises we were and could no longer keep their cocker spaniel. That was all Wally needed to hear; was it because he was becoming increasingly childlike that he wanted some small, encompassable creature to sleep next to him and lick his face? (I couldn't say to him that it was clear that Arden was far too depressed for these duties. I don't think I could even see that myself, in the crisis of those days, when I was trying to hold a collapsing house together.) We agreed. I went to pick up little Dino, but on the front

stoop, Jimmi and Tony told me they'd changed their minds, and, of course, I was glad for them that they couldn't let their animal go. But I knew how disappointed Wally would be, and on the way home I found myself pulling off the highway to the shelter, and before I knew it, here I was, on my knees on the concrete floor by the pen, in over my head.

He was, of course, much bigger than a cocker spaniel, but he seemed the calmest, dreamiest dog, the perfect candidate for the required sleeping and licking duties.

He gazed at me steadily, still thumping, and then rose again, walked back over, and put the beautiful weight of his head in my hands.

That did it.

On the way out, I'd learn that this admirable tranquility was the result of sedation; Beau had been neutered, as was the shelter's policy, and he was just waking up. Never mind, I said yes anyway and was told the next step would be to bring Arden over to meet him; the shelter wanted to be sure they'd get along.

Back home, I'm ablaze with the news: Wally's excited, if a little bit uncertain about the size of the new arrival, who isn't going to be the cuddly small thing he'd anticipated. My friends think I've lost my mind: *You're taking care of a man who can't get out of bed and you're adopting a golden retriever?* They do have a point, but there's a certain dimension of experience at which the addition of any other potential stress simply doesn't matter anymore. Oh, say the already crazed, why not?

Arden, as ever, is happy to go for a ride and sits in the passenger seat taking in the landscape, turning to me from time to time, while we drive the half hour to Brewster. It occurs to me that I should be a little nervous about taking him to a shelter, given his history—does he remember the smell, the texture of animal anxiety in the air? If he does, he doesn't indicate it. He waits in the car while I go in and, with an attendant, bring Beau outside to a small, grassy corral where the two can run around together. The attendant, sturdy in her jeans and hooded sweatshirt, watches from just outside the gate; she wants to see that the two dogs get along. Which they do, just fine, racing around on the grass, greeting and tussling, though I can tell that, in fact, Beau's high energy—he's just been let OUT—is a little startling to Arden. And playing with a stranger in a neutral, outdoor space is quite another thing than said stranger actually getting into your car with you, but I tell the attendant all is completely well. Arden waits in the front seat while I sign the papers and pay the twenty-five dollars, and then I bring our new dog to the car, where he leaps inside and begins merrily bouncing about. Arden commences a quiet, throaty growl, far more threatening than any louder demonstration. I drive out of the parking lot very quickly, my family suddenly one member larger.

Wally's just about to eat his lunch when we arrive. Nancy, the home health aide, has made him a bacon, lettuce, and tomato sandwich with mayonnaise, and when we come hurtling into the room, Beau jumps onto the bed in wild greeting, licks Wally's face exuberantly while Wally laughs and laughs, and then the untutored creature simply consumes the lunch off the plate, every last bite.

Some things I learn about Beau immediately: The pads on the bottom of his feet are pink and soft as human skin, and seem hardly to have touched the earth. He has been living in a crate. He lacks, almost entirely, what

psychologists call "impulse control." He doesn't know his name, or any other word. He is no Saluki mix but a starving retriever, and if he's three years old, he certainly hasn't been fed much, as he immediately begins a process of doubling in size. His appetite is prodigious, boundless. Most days, we walk along the town beach. Off-season, especially in the morning or early evening, when no one's about, dogs walk there off-leash, taking delight in waves and wrack line, splashing into the water. Beau is unnervingly interested in the backs of the houses that front the water, sniffing out more to eat. One day, we're walking past the back of Saint Mary's of the Harbor, where an early church supper has just ended, and the leftovers are being tossed down onto the sand for the squawking seagulls. Who would have thought that a retriever would love baked beans? Vast amounts of beans, pounds of them. I know I should intervene, but I'm so startled by his ardor, by the prospect of this neglected youth suddenly having *enough*, a rich, steaming demonstration of enough, that I can't help but just let him go.

Arden is visibly stunned, albeit too gentlemanly not to be accomodating, and I am consoled in knowing I haven't just displaced him or made him feel put out because he is clearly, beneath a certain level of mature exasperation, *interested* in Beau. Who is this obstreperous thing? Taking up a great deal of space, socially clueless, but even to Arden, it appears, charming. I know because on his first day in the house, Beau commences a game with Arden, the sort of head-wrestling Arden used to do as a puppy, years ago, with his pit bull pal in the weeds back by the railroad tracks. Arden and Beau lie on the floor, heads close to one another, and their teeth flash as they lunge and nip and make horrible noises, a pair of wolverines in heat; they more or less playfully attempt to bite each other on the neck, each trying to deflect the other's teeth, so that often the big ivories click against each other—if teeth could spark, the house would have burned down. Sometimes the matter gets out of hand, even for them, and there's a yelp and retreat, then in a minute they're back at it again till neither one of them can hold their eyes open.

When we have to rent a hospital bed, I push an old single iron one up against it so we can still sleep together. If some of the people who came to help us out are quietly horrified that both beds are full of retrievers—well, so be it. We've made an island, a small, very full home.

Beau's never really still until he simply keels over, usually in bed and curls himself into a ball like a golden hedgehog, tumbling headlong into sleep. If I'm worn out with him, if I'm entertaining the notion that maybe I've made a big mistake, all such thoughts vanish when I look at that face, awake or asleep. I have never thought of myself as a patient person, but some new reserve seems to be appearing within me; I can sit with Wally and talk about nothing, remind him gently when he's watched the same episode of *The Golden Girls* three times in a row and found it equally funny every time, tease him about his appetite, laugh with him when he can't find the words he wants.

And I have a bottomless reserve of tolerance for Beau. If he wanders out onto Bradford Street, where in the off-season people drive a ridiculous number of miles per hour, I'm terrified, but it happens so many times I have to begin to negotiate with the panic I feel when he runs; this is part of his wildness, I tell myself, part of who he is, and if he does get hurt, I'll have done everything I can. But, in fact, he seems to have a charmed life, though once or twice cars must slam on the brakes for him and for me right behind, chasing him across the middle of the road. When I catch up with him, I try to firmly communicate that this was a terrible idea, but, in truth, that wagging tail dissolves both fear and anger.

When we go out the back door for a walk, or come in from one, whenever he's off his leash, he's fond of leaping the stockade fence—no mean height—to head for the garbage cans behind us at a little rental compound called Julia's Cottages for Two. I look for him until I find him, usually in Julia's trash, gobbling some old chicken bones, and then he looks up at me and starts swishing that plumy tail back and forth like crazy, all happiness. He looks at me with the plainest, pleased gaze, and what's to be upset about?

This is all a bit like a famous old joke. A man goes to a rabbi for help. I'm miserable, he says, my life is unbearable. What's the matter, asks the rabbi? I have a tiny house, an angry wife, six children, almost nothing to eat, my feet hurt, what can I do? The rabbi says, without raising an eyebrow, Get a goat. This sounds crazy to the man, but this rabbi's reputed to be very wise, so he does it anyway. The next week, he comes back to the rabbi. Help me, he says, the goat is a disaster! The goat eats our clothes, takes up all the space in our little house, my wife is furious, it steps on my feet, what can I do? The rabbi says, absolutely calmly, Get rid of the goat. Next week, the man comes back and says, Oh, rabbi, thank you, my life is wonderful now!

The difference is I love the goat.

One day, when he's sacked out next to Wally, his back close to Wally's hips, I see my lover lift his right hand—the hand he can't use to feed himself anymore—and bring it through the air, with intense deliberation, to rest on Beau's golden flanks. I take a picture of that gesture because that's the way I want to remember him. Maybe the last thing he ever did with that hand, I don't know. The gesture perhaps not so much for Beau himself—the bounding, confused, happy thing—as toward all he represented: possibility, beginning, potential sweetness, vitality. Dear man reaching to the world: how I want to go when I do.